12/5

14 MAY 2003
OLD ST.
FIRST CIRCLE

SOLOVIEV

The Man and the Prophet

EUGENIA GOURVITCH

SOLOVIEV

The Man and the Prophet

RUDOLF STEINER PRESS

Translated by J. Deverill
Edited by J. W. Ernst and Dr. A. Welburn

© **Rudolf Steiner Press, Sussex, 1992**

ISBN: 1 85584 165 7

Typeset by Imprint, Crawley Down
Printed and Bound in Great Britain

CONTENTS

PREFACE

This book is an accurate record of the thoughts of E. B. Gourvitch resulting from her many years study of the works of V. Soloviev. For most of her life she read and re-read Soloviev's compositions, poetry and correspondence as well as reminiscences about him. Eugenia gave whole series of lectures on themes mentioned in this book and loved to expound her views in discussion. Unfortunately, no record was kept of most of the lectures, and for a long time she delayed starting this book. Only in the last year of her life did she apply herself seriously to this task, but had no time to revise the text. She died within three days of completing the manuscript in Russian.

Two days before her death Eugenia handed the manuscript to her brother so that he might translate it into German, having earlier asked John Deverill to make an English translation.

After reading the text it became clear to us that it was essential to edit the book, and that the anthroposophical background of thought needed to be clarified by means of certain additions as well as commentary and explanations. We therefore approached Eugenia's old friend, the anthroposophist Wolfgang Ernst, who readily accepted the responsibility.

John Deverill, Alexander Gourvitch

FOREWORD

by The Editor

The preparation of this manuscript has been an extraordinary task for me. The author began to write down her thoughts only after relinquishing her responsibilities as managing director of an important industrial enterprise. She then had little more than two years life remaining and she knew that there was no time to lose.

In such circumstances an author's style often assumes a special character or 'end of life' style, when only the most important points are defined, facts are dealt with shortly, and matters of secondary importance, associations and explanations excluded. Logical structure also suffers because the author is in a hurry. First drafts always have these characteristics but usually the author has time to smooth the roughness, bring order to the text, correct deficiencies and add any necessary explanations. If the author dies, as in this case, before the work can be completed, somebody must assume responsibility for editing, which for such a book can be extremely complicated, involving, as it were, a dialogue with the deceased.

Over the last twenty-five years I have visited London almost annually where I often engaged in long discussions with Eugenia about Soloviev, the Holy Sophia and Anthroposophy. From these conversations I can therefore deduce what the author had in mind, and can also remember quite precisely what she said on various points dealt with in the book. Thus I am in a position to rectify some of the shortcomings of the 'end of life' style, smooth the roughness, repair omissions and enlarge on remarks. In other words, the editor has had to insert into the text both material originally excluded as well as comment. [So that the reader may clearly identify editorial additions they are printed between square brackets, as is this sentence.] Rearrangements of the order in the text are not specifically mentioned.

Eugenia Gourvitch's book about Soloviev deals with three aspects, to which specialists in Soloviev have so far paid little heed: Soloviev as a clairvoyant, as a poet and as a man. All the recollections of his contemporaries, his letters, his poems and articles are pervaded by this image, but almost all the authors of biographies of Soloviev concentrate on the featureless portrayal of Soloviev as a philosopher.

Eugenia Gourvitch was born exactly five years after Soloviev's death, and on the same date. She attached great significance to this. It seemed to her to require that she should devote herself to Soloviev as a *person*, delineating the character traits of his personality, correcting various blemishes which had appeared on his portrait, and explaining a whole range of oddities in his make-up which can be understood only after many years of patient study in depth. These studies showed the author how very great indeed is the significance of this spirit, who in Russia apparently has the influence of an unseen immortal.

Soloviev is the man of the future. His real world significance will become clear now that it is again possible to print his books in Russia. Even now, to judge from various communications, Soloviev is one of the most popular writers of Samizdat, and in the hidden Russia he already has the influence of one of the greatest personalities. Understanding the profound spiritual significance of Soloviev, E. B. Gourvitch saw in him a prophet of the future, and in testimony she wrote this book.

J. W. Ernst

REFERENCES

In the text references to Soloviev's writings are made in the following way:

Works   Complete works of Vladimir Sergeyvich Soloviev, edited and annotated by S. M. Soloviev and E. L. Radlov. Second edition — St. Petersburg, 1908 — 1913, in 10 volumes in the Russian language.

Letters   The letters of Vladimir Sergeyvich Soloviev, edited by E. L. Radlov. St. Petersburg, 1908 — 1911, in 3 volumes in the Russian language.

Letters 1923 The letters of Vladimir Soloviev, edited by E. L. Radlov, St. Petersburg 1923.

Poems   Vladimir Soloviev, Poems, 7th edition. Moscow 1921, in Russian.

References to the lectures and works of Rudolf Steiner are principally translated from the German texts, published in Dornach from 1955 under the general title *Rudolf Steiner Gesamtausgabe, Rudolf Steiner Verlag, Dornach*. The passage from *Geschichtliche Symptomatologie* is translated from the 1942 edition, edited by Marie Steiner. The footnotes give the volume of the *Gesamtausgabe*, prefixed by the letters G.A. The page numbers depend on the edition, but in all volumes the lectures are identified by the dates on which they were given, in chronological order.

In the English version the Matthews system of transliteration has been used for Russian names, except where this might result in confusion with traditional English spellings.

Chapter One

SOLOVIEV —
PHILOSOPHER, POET AND WRITER

I remember how, in my early youth, as a pupil at the Tenishevsky Classical Grammar School, we made a visit to Moscow. We had been invited to the First Grammar School to listen to a lecture about Moscow to be read by Professor Lapshin, if I am not mistaken. But instead of a lecture on Moscow he asked us if we knew 'who had walked these very floor-boards?'. Receiving a negative reply, he named Vladimir Sergeyevich Soloviev, and understanding from the confusion of our teacher that we knew very little about him, he lectured us on Vladimir Soloviev.

Even earlier, in childhood, influenced by Soloviev's portrait which I had seen in the museum of Alexander III (now the Museum of Russian Art) I had asked at dinner 'Who is this Vladimir Soloviev?'. And I remember the radiant face of my grandmother, who knew comparatively little of Russian literature and philosophy, saying in reply: 'He was a very great man'. Recalling Soloviev people likened his face to that of one inspired. This was not related to Soloviev's ideas or to his poetry but mainly to his personality. There were those who cared little for his philosophy or verse, but I have never heard or read of anyone who did not esteem his personality.

My book contains no exposition of the philosophy of Vladimir Soloviev because so many books have been written about it by others and because he himself set out his thoughts with unsurpassed clarity, logic and beauty of language, on which improvement would be impossible.

Furthermore, Soloviev's philosophy was not, in my opinion, the most important aspect of his life and work. Andrey Bely writes of this in his *Arabesques*. [1] 'He told his brother that his mission in life did not consist of writing books on philosophy; that all his writings were only a prologue to his subsequent activities'. And in his letter of March 1900 to Anna Schmidt Soloviev he also related something in the same vein. He described the dream of

---

1 Andrey Bely, *Arabesques*, Munich 1969 (in Russian), p. 394 .

an old lady long since dead: 'She saw herself receive a letter from me, written in my usual handwriting, which she called "spider's feet" ! Reading it with interest she noticed that folded inside was yet another letter written on fine paper. Opening it she saw the words beautifully inscribed in gold ink and at the same time heard my voice saying: "This is my real letter, but wait to read it", and then she saw me enter in person, bent beneath the weight of an enormous sack full of copper coins. I took several coins out of the sack and threw them one by one on the floor, saying: "After the copper we will come to the golden words" '. [2] This means that at the end of his life Soloviev himself was of this opinion.

When Milyukov wrote an article expounding Soloviev's ideas and categorizing him as a Slavophile, Soloviev wrote: 'As to those things Milyukov calls "my ideas", surely it is not I who invented Christianity or insisted that its precepts be put into practice?'. [3]

2 Vladimir Soloviev, *Letters IV*, St. Petersburg 1923, p. 11.
3 *Works*, Vol. VI, p. 427.

Chapter Two

THE PROBLEM OF THE CHURCH

It may seem strange to be writing about the Church in these times when most churches are empty; when for more than a century all manner of 'scientific' authorities have 'known' that there is no historical evidence for the existence of Jesus of Nazareth, still less of Jesus Christ; when He who is described in the works of His disciples and evangelists has been subjected to 'scientific' psychoanalysis and even children and the semi-literate among us affirm that the evangelists were incapable even of transcribing the first Gospel conscientiously, and that consequently the four Gospels conflict and contradict each other to such an extent that the Catholic Church, knowing this, once forbade their reading other than in Latin and even now continues to discourage it.

Nevertheless I raise this question, and write on this theme, because the problem lives on, as crucial as ever, in many hearts, and because in different places one person after another testifies to having seen or having had experience of the very real presence of Jesus Christ.

Since the last century people have been having presentiments or experience in one form or another of the *initiatives* of Christ, but, unfortunately, when the moment of contact with Him or His emissaries is past, they seek a repetition of that moment in tradition, that is — in the past, and not ahead, where He will always be found. This is what happened in Germany with F. Schlegel, the philosopher of Romanticism, converted to Catholicism towards the end of his life, and in Russia with Berdyaev, Karsavin and others. Vladimir Soloviev had the same temptation, but successfully overcame it.

When the reality of the experience, [arising in the higher plane of cognizance] which man never ascribes to himself but always considers as a gift from the spiritual world, pales or passes, man seeks to restore it in his intellect. But in their intellect people are egoists; they do not want to listen but to assert. This leads to aggressiveness, insecurity and even cruelty.

Of course one cannot really blame people for striving towards organization. When a person grasps, however remotely, the true embodiment of spiritual life on earth, he feels his soul expand and his wings unfold; his hands stretch out towards fellow souls with the same experience; he sees spiritual life in the image of the 'Holy Sophia' and strives to achieve her embodiment in this world, and the vision of the Holy Grail appears before his eyes. But the fact is that the Grail is not yet with us, it is only descending to earth; the Christianity of the Grail desirous of embodiment exists, but the Grail's servants have been so few. A model for the temple of the Grail could well have been the Church of St Sophia in Constantinople (now Istanbul), whose vaults are a series of inverted vessels interdependent and interlocking and so united with the others in one glorious whole.

Approaching the end of my life, I personally do not favour any organization which attempts to organize the religious or spiritual life of people unless both organizers and organized have attained a very high level of spiritual and human attainment. However I can understand the endeavour of people to unite in their spiritual and emotional experience and actions.

I know that in unity with others man is more powerful than alone. But I also cannot but observe that if those who unite are not genuine servants of the Grail they succumb to temptation and use their power for selfish goals rather than for the identification of Christ's impulse.

Of course, as I have said, in that moment of great happiness accompanying the experience of Christ, man is inspired to unite with others, but by the slightest hint of egoism or ambition the unity is spoilt and nullified. [Egoism and ambition find expression even in the exaggerated preoccupation with clerical rites and ceremonies rather than an inner spiritual effort to approach Christ.] However, people brought up in the Christian tradition may overcome these impediments [by resisting exaggeration of the importance of external ceremonies]. But it is the height of foolishness for those brought up in Jewish, Muslim or atheistic traditions, such as Marxism, suddenly to start crossing themselves. They will never find Christ in Church.

In general the true reality of temples and churches reposes in art. Dogmas, the subjects of theological argument among clerics and only accessible to intellect, have little meaning for mankind; whereas art, filling the churches — the paintings, sculpture, the architecture itself of temples and churches, music sounding within them, mystery plays preserving the memory and feeling of Christ — has inspired mankind since time immemorial. When the Puritans began to destroy art in the churches religious feeling began to wither, and now in our time the churches are empty. However, the world can no longer sustain itself spiritually on past and ancient classic art alone. As new impulses are born they appear and find expression in art.

Apart from very exceptional people most see Christ and the Mother of Jesus in terms of pictures, and in this sense our religious guides were the great artists, icon painters and sculptors.

It would be wrong to think that artists and sculptors did what they were ordered to do by popes, cardinals and bishops. These, of course, exploited for their own glory the talent and inspiration of the artists but were unable to give spiritual or artistic substance to the artistic creations but only admire them like the rest. The artists themselves in truth were our religious leaders. Would we be at all able to visualize the features of Christ or His Mother if we had never seen Leonardo da Vinci's 'Last Supper', Raphael's 'Sistine Madonna', Michelangelo's 'Pietà', or the representations of Sophia in Russian churches? In this sense one may say that while the official Church anathematized, fought for power, argued about dogma and burned people at the stake, true inspiration came from the artists, sculptors and minstrels.

If we were to ask different people what they understood by 'Church', we would get very different replies. Some churchgoers would say the 'Church' is the building where people pray, or the place for baptisms, weddings and funerals, or where sermons are preached. Some Catholics would say: 'It is the organization of Christians'. Anti-Catholics would say: 'It is a political organization' and recall its dreadful history. The majority of both Roman Catholics and Orthodox Christians would say the Church is Christianity itself and affirm the impossibility of being a Christian without baptism in Church. Catholics would refer to Christ's words: 'Upon this Rock I will build my Church, and the Gates of Hell shall not prevail against it'. Protestants would also quote Christ's words 'For where two or three are gathered together in My name, there am I in the midst of them'. These last often fail to recognize how difficult it is for people to gather together in His name.

The highest authority of the Catholic and Orthodox Churches is the Councils. [These are the assemblies of Christians in His name. The Orthodox Church recognizes only the first seven

Councils, which met in the first nine centuries after Christ's birth. This was the period when eastern and western churches were unified, and a universal church, embracing the whole world, supposedly still existed. But even in the second century this universal church had expelled the Gnostics, and in the third the Manichaeans who were widespread in the near and far East and also in Africa. In the fourth century the Arians were expelled, and in the fifth the Nestorians, and the Syrian, Persian and Indian churches. In other words there had never been a universal church. The last so-called universal Council, the eighth, held in Constantinople in AD 869, was not recognized by the Eastern Church. It was recognized only by the Catholic Church. Since then there have been a whole series of exclusively Roman Catholic Councils, the last in the 1960's]. The prototype of the Councils was, apparently, Pentecost. [The Councils were looked upon as repetitions of this event, described in the New Testament as the first Pentecost.] What happened then? Let us turn our attention to Acts 1. 14: 'These all' (that is the twelve apostles) 'continued with one accord in prayer and supplication, with the women, and Mary the Mother of Jesus, and with his brethren'. Note that the Mother of Jesus was with them. The second chapter describes what happened during Pentecost (Acts 2, 1 — 6):

And when the day of Pentecost was fully come, they were all with one accord in one place. And suddenly there came a sound from heaven as of a rushing mighty wind, and it filled all the house where they were sitting. And there appeared unto them cloven tongues like as of fire, and it sat upon each of them. And they were are filled with the Holy Ghost, and began to speak with other tongues, as the Spirit gave them utterance. And there were dwelling at Jerusalem Jews, devout men, out of every nation under heaven. Now when this was noised abroad, the multitude came together and were confounded, because that every man heard them speak in his own language ...

[This is completely the reverse of what happened during the construction of the Tower of Babylon (Genesis 11, 1 — 9). 'And the whole earth was of one language, and of one speech ... And they said, Go to, let us build us a city and a tower, whose top may reach unto heaven ... And the Lord said ... Let us go down, and there confound their language, that they may not understand one another's speech'.]

Yet what was happening in the Councils even before their official recognition, when Christians were still being persecuted from time to time by the Roman authorities? Even in AD 303, under the Emperor Diocletian, there was cruel persecution and torture of Christians. The Councils engaged in endless arguments about dogma and their best people were accused of heresy. In truth the arguments had little to do with dogma, an intellectual matter which does not arouse passion, whereas the Councils were emotional and preoccupied with national interests and disputes over power. [During the Councils ideas were thrown into confusion, just as at Babylon in its time languages were confused.] At the beginning of the fourth century the Emperor Constantine, a typical Roman emperor, preparing for battle with his rival Maxentius, dreamt that he saw a cross in the sky, with the inscription 'By this thou shalt conquer'. He had crosses emblazoned on his standards and subsequently gained a great victory over Maxentius. In fact most of the Germans in the army of Maxentius were Arian Christians who would not fight against the Cross.* Thus Constantine realized that Christianity was a great power which he could use for Rome and for himself. Constantine was never a Christian, and the story that he had been baptized shortly before his death by Eusebius of Nicomedia is of a later date and quite unproven. (What sort of a Christian Eusebius of Nicomedia was may be judged from the views on Christianity he instilled in his ward and nephew, the future Emperor Julian, 'The Apostate').

Constantine's statue, standing in the Forum with the statues of other Roman emperors, had its head superimposed on the torso of Mars, his real god. How little Constantine's vision of the

* It must be said that the legend that the Germans were Arians is very dubious. Until the Council of Nicaea, Arius was a little known Egyptian presbyter and it is very unlikely that he would have been able to convert the Germans to his following by AD 312. Right up until the present this historical enigma has remained unsolved. The future development of the Germans was the main theme of the arguments at the Council of Nicaea: whether they should be allowed to develop independently, maintaining their own cultural identity, or whether they should be compelled to associate with the cultural development of the Mediterranean peoples. Arius seems to have defended the more liberal approach: let them develop as they wish.

Cross had converted him to Christianity can be gauged from the fact that following the victory over Maxentius he killed two of his sons. He also killed his own son. [In 324 Constantine made Christianity the religion of the Roman Empire; in 325, a year later, he called the Council of Nicaea; in 326 he killed his own son, and in 327, just another year later, he killed his wife after 20 years of marriage.] And this was the man the Church canonized and named 'the Great' and 'apostolic'!

So at the behest of Constantine and at government expense the bishops and their assistants and servants assembled for the Council of Nicaea in AD 325. The Council opened only when Constantine arrived. The well-known religious historian Eusebius Pamphylius wrote that the Emperor shone with gold and precious stones and 'resembled the Archangel Michael'. No wonder the only recently persecuted Christians were greatly impressed by the Emperor's attention. The official reason for the Council was the dispute between two Egyptian clerics — Arius and Athanasius. Constantine of course was indifferent to the outcome, but having decided that Christianity meant power he did not wish this power dissipated. [The argument was as to whether 'Christ, the Son of God', was essentially 'God the Father', that is — a unity, which would be difficult to comprehend — or whether He was His Son in the sense that any son resembles his father whilst remaining different. This would make Christ one god among others.] His personal friends were Arians and Arianism was generally more easily understood. Nevertheless, after long arguments, anathema was pronounced on Arius and Arianism and Arians were banished from the Emperor's domains. Christianity was proclaimed the official religion of the Roman Empire, although pagans were not discriminated against. [The dispute did not end here. In 336 Constantine rehabilitated the teachings of Arius, and despite his death that same year Arianism was obviously predominating, especially in the eastern half of the Roman empire. Constantine died the following year, in 337, but the dispute between the two Christian movements continued throughout the whole of the fourth century.]

Let us return to the meaning of 'Church'. In the ancient world of Greece and Rome there was no Church as such. There were various Mysteries and complete tolerance of different cults based on spiritual activities. They all differed between one temple and another, between one town and another. Participants and devotees of the Mysteries judged their actions and their religious results by their spiritual content, whereas the ordinary people and the uninitiated followed a popular religion. [Such a difference in approach was accepted and the only condition acknowledged by all was the respect to be accorded to all temples. The harassment of Christians in imperial Rome arose from the fact that they refused to acknowledge the imperium as a Mystery and the emperor as one of the gods. This was resented as the utmost intolerance on the part of the Christians and provoked their persecution.]

Nor did Jews possess a church, although there existed a preparatory stage. Time and time again they built and rebuilt a sanctuary with the implicit demand that it be recognized by all Jews as sole source of religion. From this derived the mobile sanctuary where the Ten Commandments were kept, probably with a few other sacred books. King Solomon built a temple. The description is in the Bible. [According to a masonic legend about the Temple, which derives from the Rosicrucians of the late Middle Ages, the construction of King Solomon's Temple was never completed. Solomon, a descendant of Abel, entrusted the architect and brass-founder Hiram (descended from Cain, according to the legend) with the construction of the building in the centre of which was to stand a brass laver, no doubt resembling the Grail. In the Old Testament it is written that the laver was cast and placed in position.] But according to the probably very ancient masonic legend the biblical text had been written *in advance*, whereas in fact when the time came to pour the casting for the laver it was unsuccessful, partly because Solomon was envious and jealous of Hiram, and partly because Hiram's three evil apprentices killed him with Solomon's connivance.

Thus the Temple was never entirely Jehovah's abode. It was destroyed by Nebuchadnezzar in 586 BC, rebuilt in 520 BC, desecrated by Antiochus Epiphanes and rededicated by Judas Maccabaeus. The third Temple was built by the evil King Herod the Great, murderer of the infants, and was destroyed by the Romans in AD 70. Of it only the Wailing Wall remains, where Jews go to pray and weep to this day. Julian the Apostate tried to rebuild the Temple but gases which appeared in the cellars frustrated this attempt. [It is possible that the Rosicrucian legend is based on Jewish legends explaining the strange fate of the Temple — the explanation as to why Jehovah failed to protect his abode.]

The Jews built many a synagogue, but never another Temple. They understood the difference. [The Temple could only be a structure uniting all. It could be created only after unification of the deeply divided personalities of Solomon and Hiram, Cain and Abel, to found the community of the Temple.] There is a Passover prayer of the Jews, which enraptured Vladimir Soloviev. It is a prayer for the restoration of the Temple. 'Almighty God, create Thy temple now and quickly, quickly in our time, as soon as possible, create it now, create it now, create it now, now and quickly create Thy temple! Merciful God, exalted God, gentle God, God the most high, blessed God, dearest God, God the infinite, God of the Israelites, create Thy temple soon, quickly, quickly, in our time, create it now, create it now, create it now, create it now, create Thy temple now and quickly.' [4]

This prayer deals of course with conversion of the whole world into a temple of God. This thought of the all-embracing Temple arose either before or at the same time as the Christian idea of the all-uniting Church but the Christians since the time of the first Council of Nicaea have come to think of Church as the community of people adhering to one dogma. They rejected those who disagreed with them and by doing so have split the Church into fragments.

[In the early Christian Church, dogmas, i.e. 'mandatory resolutions', were held to be the decision of the Councils, assemblies of prominent Christians bishops, scholars, monks, etc., who following discussions and by majority vote had to decide on what was 'truth' for Christianity. This procedure was founded on the 'infallibility' of majority Council decisions, these, like the Council itself, being 'inspired' by the Holy Ghost, just as the apostles and the women were inspired at Pentecost. It is this triple equation — 'Council majority — Council — Pentecost' that is the foundation of the basic dogma, on which rest all other dogmas. This basic dogma however is only an analogy, without internal or external justification, and the basic dogma has never been declared as such at any Council.]

This then is the rather optimistic hope, that this is the basis for the belief of the Church in dogmas, a somewhat unreliable basis considering that all Councils past and present have proved to be political events with an admixture of intrigue.

4. *Works*, Vol. 4, p. 147.

Chapter Three

THE THREE MEETINGS

A man whose destiny was bound up with the problem of the Church and the questions of its reality lived in Russia from 1853 to 1900 — the philosopher, publicist and poet, Vladimir Sergeyevich Soloviev. He was born in Moscow on 16 January 1853 and died on 12 August 1900 at Uskoye, the estate of Prince Trubetskoy. He was born prematurely, like St. Paul, and under the sign of Aquarius. To both these circumstances he apparently attached importance and in presenting his book *The Justification of Good* to friends he inscribed the dedication:

> I appeared in this world under the sign of Aquarius;
> So drink up bravely this water I bring;
> Not missed, but found in the wilderness,
> Where the rock of truth gives birth to this spring. [5]

And in one of his letters apologizing to a friend for discourteous silence in the presence of a lady of their acquaintance with whom he had been travelling by train, he wrote that he had been born two months prematurely and had been unable to give voice, but could only open his mouth like a young sparrow. [6]

The famous philosopher, the creator of the Russian philosophical language, the brilliant orator and poet, inspiration and teacher of Blok and Bely, felt he was unable to express his innermost thoughts. Hence his poetry is mingled with jokes, hence he always felt himself alone, and that there was no place for his muse 'between the two enemy camps' and wrote:

> The rule is so : all the better in the fog,
> For proximity is painful or funny,
> And one can't avoid the double frontiers
> Of ringing laughter and dumb sobbing,
> Universe created harmony.[7]

5. *Letters*, Vol. I, p. 264.
6. *Letters*, Vol. I, p. 150.
7. *Poems*, p. 72.

Rudolf Steiner said that every child chooses his or her own parents; Vladimir Sergeyevich Soloviev chose well. In this respect he had everything he could have wanted. He was the son of the eminent Russian historian Sergey Mikhailovich Soloviev, for many years Professor and Dean of Moscow University, and himself the son of a priest — Father Mikhail Vasilyevich Soloviev. V. S. Soloviev's mother was Ukrainian, the grand-niece of a famous Ukrainian philosopher, Grigory Skovoroda, mystic and peripatetic preacher, who journeyed through many lands studying mystical, masonic and theosophical ideas. He wandered through the Ukraine telling his compatriots about different Christian teachings.

Soloviev combined the conscientiousness and erudition of his father, the good spirits and kindliness of his grandfather, and the inclination towards mysticism of his Ukrainian forebear.

At the age of nine, while in church, Soloviev had a vision he only decided to write about towards the end of his life, in semi-humorous verse in his poem 'Three Meetings'.[8] Here is the beginning of this poem describing the first meeting:

THREE MEETINGS
(Moscow, London, Egypt — 1862 / 1875 / 1876)

A POEM

> Having triumphed in advance over death,
> And conquered with love the chains of time,
> I will not summon you, eternal mistress,
> But have no doubt you hear my modest rhyme.
>
> Disbelieving the illusions of the world,
> I probed beneath the rough crust of matter,
> And touched the imperishable mantle,
> And recognized the radiance of the Godhead.
>
> Did you not thrice surrender to my gaze?
> Not through intellectual musings, not at all,
> But in warning, or to help, or in reward,
> Your image answered my soul's call.

8. *Poems*, p. 170.

I

The first time; how long ago that was!
Thirty-six years have passed by since
My childish soul unexpectedly experienced
The ache of love and obscure dreams.

I was nine years old; she was nine as well. *
' 'Twas a May night in Moscow' as Fet put it.
I said I loved her. Silence. Oh my God !
There must be a rival. He would answer for it.

Duel! Duel! Mass on Ascension Day.
In a stream of fervid torment my heart seethes.
' ... banish ... worldly ... cares ...'
The words draw out, fade, die in silence.

The altar is there; but where the priest? The deacon?
Where the thronging worshipping congregation?
My passion ? Withered and gone without a trace.
Blue all around. Blue within my soul.

Blue pierced with shafts of gold.
In your hand a flower from other realms,
You stood with radiant smile,
Nodded to me and were hidden in the mist.

And childish love from me departed,
My heart to worldliness was blinded,
And my German governess sadly repeated,
'Volodyenka, you are so stupid!'.

* The 'she' on this line was an ordinary little girl and nothing to do with
the 'eternal mistress' of the introduction. V.S.

After this experience it was as if the vision had fallen asleep within
him. In the company of boisterous friends he concerned himself
with frogs and tadpoles, played at ghosts and frightened holidaymakers, later on to his father's dismay becoming engrossed in
the works of Renan and similar writers critical of the Bible and

becoming quite blasphemously iconoclastic in some aspects of his own behaviour. This went on until he was about eighteen.

If his childish feelings returned he apparently gave little sign of them. As has been mentioned before, he found it difficult to express his innermost feelings and when he did so often included an element of self-mockery. But apparently he never forgot his vision. 'The rough crust of matter', the illusion, sloughed off and beneath he 'touched the imperishable mantle' cloaking the world soul.

This is what Soloviev wrote to his cousin Katya Romanova in 1872 [9] after he had been reading science at university for several years. His cousin was also intent on studying the natural sciences, but he persuaded her that this was pointless. 'I am of the opinion', he wrote, 'that to study the insubstantial phantoms of external appearances is even sillier than living by empty illusions. Most importantly, this "science" cannot achieve its goal. People look into microscopes, dissect miserable creatures, boil up some muck or other in their retorts, and imagine they are studying nature. Such asses should have their foreheads inscribed:

> Nature and its beauty
> Are not to be uncovered
> Machines will not identify
> What thy spirit should have discovered.

> Instead of nature they embrace dead bones!'

It is interesting that Soloviev should quote this quatrain from Goethe's *Faust*, that is, from the writer who sought and found his path through nature to the eternal feminine. However, Soloviev uses a mistranslation of Goethe's words which read, in the translation by W. H. Van der Smissen:

> Nature hath secrets in the light of day,
> Of her enshrouding veil none may bereave her,
> What to your mind she deigns not to display
> Ye cannot force from her with screw or lever.

Characteristically Goethe implies that nature cannot be forced to reveal her secrets to man; equally characteristically Soloviev insists that the initiative is with man to understand nature through his own spirit.

9 *Letters*, Vol. 3, p. 64 (letter to E. K. Selevina, née Romanova).

Everything became repugnant to him and he went through a spiritual crisis, ceased to study and failed his examinations. [Even at this time when Soloviev was as yet only half aware of it, Christianity was for him not just a theory, but its realization in life. Christ stood everywhere before him as a mighty conceptual entity, illuminating and supporting life. Later Soloviev realized that this could not be so for non-Christians, who needed to be shown Christ as the life force. Self-professed Christians who failed to see Christ in this form were guilty of muddled thinking. Therefore Soloviev saw it as his prime responsibility to prepare for Christ's victory and to introduce the God-man to philosophy.]

In his third year at university Soloviev left the natural science faculty and moved to the philosophical, at the same time putting in voluntary attendance at the theological academy. Graduating brilliantly in philosophy he was outstandingly successful in defending his Master's thesis on 'The Crisis of Western Philosophy' prior to his appointment as lecturer in Moscow University. His thesis and its defence raised a furore. The Slavophiles gave him the warmest of welcomes. One professor wrote to Soloviev's father: 'Russia is to be congratulated on this fine scholar'. When he started his course of lectures, the students, who at that time were very materialistically minded, were ready to heckle this Christian philosopher (a rare combination at the time and one which leftish youth identified with the extreme right). But they were won over by his reasoning and even more so by his personality, which was always at one with what he said. His lectures were so successful that they had to be held in the Great Hall of the University; students from other faculties attended and the normal lecture rooms were too small to accommodate the audiences.

In 'The Crisis of Western Philosophy' Soloviev criticized the thinking behind western philosophical trends, and tried to show how, if followed to their logical conclusions, they must end in positivism and materialism or in meaningless idealism. He tried to bring these tendencies together in a synthesis, affirming that this synthesis was religion. This was his first appearance in public, and in university circles such an approach provoked loud and disdainful criticism.

One must bear in mind the position of the intelligentsia in Russia at that time. There were two movements — Western and Slavophiles, bitterly fighting each other. Their quarrels continued throughout the nineteenth century, and despite the fact that both movements originated from the same social circles and the same Hegelian school, by the start of the 1880's the enmity between them was so fierce and had taken on such a personal nature that they refused even to speak to each other. Both movements had arisen from a recognition of the same need, and among the representatives of each movement were numbered some of the most distinguished personalities of Russian society.

The situation of Russia in those days was frightful, with the Russian people living in semi-slavery. This fact was explained in different ways and the problem was therefore approached differently. The Westerners expected a solution through the greatest possible influence of Europe, its technology and democracy, radically represented by socialism. All misfortunes they thought derived from the ignorance of the people, and enlightenment could only come from the West. The influence of the Russian Orthodox Church and Russian monastic culture was ruinous and all good came as it were from Auguste Comte, Buechner and natural science.

On the other hand, the Slavophiles counted as positive and beneficial precisely those forces reckoned pernicious by the Westerners — popular faith and Christianity. They sought for a forgotten treasure of folk culture in the hope that from it they might acquire greater energy and virtue than from servile imitation of the West. They thought Russia had lost her way because Peter the Great had scornfully prohibited the development of popular culture. The intelligentsia were thought to know nothing about this treasure, but the memory was believed to have been preserved among the common folk and it was necessary to learn from them.

To put it simply, in Russia of those days it was possible to make a career in either camp. The Slavophiles enjoyed the support of government circles, occupied important government appointments and published weighty journals. The Westerners, for their part, were the generally accepted representatives of youth, and, although sometimes persecuted, in the eyes of radical young people wore martyr's crowns.

In his twenty-first year, after finishing his course of lectures and surrounded by an aura of popularity and academic glory, Soloviev was sent abroad at his own request to visit the British

Museum, nominally to lecture on Buddhism. In fact, as he admitted towards the end of his life in the same poem 'Three Meetings', he read everything he could about 'Her'. ['She' for Soloviev was the same superior being who had appeared to him when he was a nine year old boy; this childhood experience had been indelibly impressed upon his mind. The 'puerile' period of his development (between the ages of 14 and 18) had, as it were, buried these experiences and impressions deep within his soul, but after growing up he tried to explain them to himself. He searched for similar experiences in others, studying the literature about this over the centuries and discovering that his experience was not unique but on the contrary was well known in the history of spiritual development. The ideal for mankind has usually been encountered in the image of a celestial feminine being. This was the basis of pre-Christian ideas of goddess-deities as well as the Christian tendency to deify the Mother of Christ. Plato saw her as the World Soul, a semi-cosmic being, and in the Middle Ages the female image is manifest in the allegories of the Seven Liberal Arts or the Five Graces. Albertus Magnus contrasted the proto-maternal figure Eve with Mary the Mother of Jesus and with Sophia — the being of the future. In the West in the Middle Ages Christianity was identified, not without some political overtones, with experience of the ideal 'church' surrounded by various mystical concepts such as with 'The Bride and Mother of Christ'.

Soloviev identified his experience with the image of Sophia, in the tradition of Eastern Christianity represented by the Novgorod and Kiev schools. 'The Novgorod ikon shows a human being, youthful, like an angel, with long hair parted in the middle, and large wings. On the head is a wreath of crowns, in the right hand — a long wand in the left — a scroll. The Kiev school shows the holy virgin with the young Jesus on her lap and her hands raised in grief, seated on the crescent moon, supported by clouds with below a podium of seven steps bearing the legends: Faith, Hope, Charity, Purity, Humility, Paradise and Glory. In both ikons the most important face is that of Jesus Christ, personifying wisdom, represented in the one ikon, that of Kiev, in the form of a "guardian angel", and in the other, that of Novgorod, in the "form of an infant".' So wrote Radlov in the Brockhaus-Efron *Encyclopaedia*, vol. 61, p. 1.

It is possible that these ikons were the main starting point for

Soloviev. As for any Russian Christian, the name Sophia was for him associated with the church of St. Sophia in Constantinople. The name Sophia first appears in the first century AD in the works of the Gnostics. But as in antiquity, so also subsequently, it has remained obscure whether Sophia is Christ's wisdom in human form or the idealization of a human personality, as with other Christian saints. Sophia has frequently been identified with the Mother of Christ for whose esoteric designation the name Sophia has been used.]

The Gnostics were a favourite subject of Soloviev's study, for many Gnostics wrote of Sophia. [One of the most significant works is *Pistis Sophia* written in Coptic. It became part of the rituals of the Ophites 'revered in the image of the Snake, and accepted as supreme Wisdom or the divine aeon of Sophia ...' writes Soloviev. [10] It is clear that Soloviev was doing everything he could to trace every possible myth about Sophia.] He also interested himself in spiritualism, doubtless trying to demonstrate empirically the reality of the spiritual world, but he soon concluded that spiritualism led nowhere, and that beneath the generally predominant charlatanry there could be no more than the tiniest grain of true magic.

Yanzhul, [11] asked by Soloviev's father to keep an eye on his unworldly son, says that he sat deeply engrossed in his own thoughts and when Yanzhul looked to see what Soloviev was reading he observed an incomprehensible cabbalistic book with strange illustrations. Judging by a later letter to Countess Tolstoy,[12] the wife of Aleksey Tolstoy, Soloviev considered that Paracelsus, Boehme and Swedenborg had experienced Sophia but She had only played about with the other mystics because of their innocence.

In any event during the six months he spent in London he felt as if surrounded by the universal soul and this determined the choice of the books he read. When considering all he managed to study in those six months, one can appreciate that this could not have been done physically, without spiritual guidance.

About his experiences in the British Museum Soloviev wrote:

10 Brockhaus-Efron *Encyclopaedia,* Vol. 44, p. 485.
11 I. I. Yanzhul — a well-known economist of that time. He was working in the British Museum at the same time as Soloviev.
12 *Letters,* Vol. 2, p. 200.

II

Years passed. Lecturer and Professor
I sped abroad for the first time.
Berlin, Hanover, Cologne in quick succession
Flashed past and disappeared from mind.

Not Paris, centre of High Society, nor Spain
Nor the brilliant colours of the east contrasted,
My dream was the British Museum,
And I was not disappointed.

How could I ever forget those blissful six months!
Not beautiful transient illusions,
Nor people, nor nature, nor passions,
But YOU alone possessed my very soul.

Let the myriad people crowd together
And the soulless buildings tower
In the grinding rumble of fiery machines!
In divine silence I am here alone.

Well of course, *cum grano salis.*
I was alone, but not misanthropic,
Visitors came to my retreat
Whose names would merit comment.

Alas, their names don't fit the verse
However well they may be known.
Let's say there were several British wizards
And two or three Moscow scholars.

I was alone in the Reading Room generally,
And God knows, believe it or not,
Unknown forces chose for me
The books about HER I should read.

And when sinful fancies led me
To take down some other tome,
Then something would compel me
In confusion to go home.

And so it happened that towards autumn
I said to HER 'O flower divine!
Thou art here. I sense it.
Why not show thyself since my childish years?'

And hardly had I thought these words
But the blue was full of gold
And HER face shone before me
But HER face alone.

And that instant was a long happiness,
To things mundane my soul was blind again,
And my babble would have seemed senseless
Had it met 'serious' ears.

III

I said 'Your face was clear to me,
But all of you I wish to see
What you vouchsafed to a small boy
You surely will not now deny'

'Go to Egypt' an inward voice replied.
No second thoughts entered my head,
Common sense was foolishly silenced.
Paris, and a train took me southwards.

Lyons, Turin, Piacenza and Ancona,
Fermi, Bari, Brindisi and then
Across the blue and choppy waters
A British steamer carried me on.

Credit and abode were found for me in Cairo
At the Abbat Hotel, now alas closed,
Comfortable, modest, the best in the world,
Russians there too, even from Moscow.

The General in No. 10 was a comfort to us all
Reminiscing of the Caucasus of old
No harm in naming him; he died long ago
And I think very kindly of him.

He was the well-known Rostislav Fadeev,
Good with his pen; retired from the army,
Knew both the tarts and the church council,
A man of infinite variety.

We met twice a day over the table d'hôte,
Where he told me many an odd story
Never at a loss for a meaningful anecdote
And even did his best with philosophy.

Meanwhile I awaited the appointed meeting
Until it came like a sweet breath of air
Late one quiet night: 'I am in the desert —
Come to me there'.

I had to walk! (From London to the Sahara
Young people cannot go for free.
In my pockets I hadn't a piastre
Having lived on tick many days already).

Where God might lead I thus set off
On foot, broke and without provender
Like uncle Vlas as wrote Nekrasov,
(Well, somehow now I've found the metre). *

You'd surely laugh as among the sands
Dressed in my overcoat and high top hat
I was taken for a devil by a frightened Bedouin
Who might very well have killed me just for that.

A council in Arabic was held noisily
As the sheikhs of the two tribes concerned
Discussed what should be done with me
Until without further words, like a slave, arms pinioned

This method of finding the metre, with the glittering example of
Pushkin in mind, is all the more excusable because the author is
more inexperienced than he is young, and is writing in discursive
verse for the first time. V. S.

I was led away, and with great courtesy
My arms released, and off they went.
I laugh with you; it comes naturally
For gods and men to laugh in retrospect.

Meanwhile, still night had fallen on the land
Coming suddenly, without preliminaries,
I felt the utter silence all around
And saw pitch black between the brilliant stars.

Reclining on the ground I watched and listened ...
A nearby jackal howled villainously
No doubt inspired by thoughts of me for dinner
And I without even a stick with me.

Never mind the jackal! It was bitterly cold
Must have been zero although so hot by day
The stars shone with piercing brilliance
And their light and the cold kept sleep at bay.

And long I lay dozing uneasily,
Until a whisper 'Sleep my poor old friend',
And I slept; then awoke suddenly
To a scent of roses from air and earth.

And in shimmering heavenly purple,
Eyes ablaze with azure fire **
You looked down like the first radiance
Of universal and creative day.

What is, what was, and what has yet to be,
All in one steady gaze encompassed
Blue seas and rivers far beneath me
Snowy mountain peaks and distant forests.

I saw all and all was one
One alone in the image of female beauty
The immeasurable within its measure
Thou alone, before me, in me.

**   Lermontov's verse. V. S.

O radiant being! This time no room for error
I saw you in the desert in entirety,
In my heart those roses will not wither,
Wherever the tides of life may carry me.

A moment! And the vision had disappeared
The sun's disc rose over the horizon
Still was the desert. My soul prayed
Hearing yet the ringing chimes of hope.

My spirits were high! But no food for two days!
My higher plane of sight faded away
Alas that spirit cannot keep its edge
But hunger is nothing to joke about, they say.

At sunrise I set off towards the Nile
Arriving home in Cairo in the evening
Still treasuring in my soul that rose-like smile
But boots with holes through which my toes were
                                                    peeping.

To the others it all seemed rather foolish
(I related all the details save the vision).
Between sips of soup the General after pausing
Fixed his eyes on me and pompously began:

'Of course intelligence is licence for stupidity,
But best by far not to abuse it,
Because understanding various kinds of insanity
Is still beyond our feeble human wit.

If it offends you to be thought at worst a madman,
Or at best to be taken for an idiot,
Then guard your tongue and say no more to anyone
About this thoroughly disreputable incident'.

And so he carried on and on about it,
But a blue mist already filled my eyes,
Life's ocean was already in retreat
Vanquished by a secret loveliness.

Though to a vain world still enslaved,
Beneath the rough crust of matter
I had glimpsed the imperishable mantle
And experienced the radiance of the Deity.

Having triumphed by prescience over death,
And conquered with dreams the chains of time
I do not summon you, eternal mistress,
But ask your pardon for my stumbling rhyme.

Note: An autumn evening and a dense forest inspired me to put into
          humorous verse this account of the most important things that
          have ever happened to me. Two days of recollection and the
          harmonies irresistibly rose in my consciousness and on the
          third day this little biography was completed and has since
          given pleasure to some poets and several ladies. V. S.

Summoned to Egypt, Soloviev lost no time in hastening there.
Why Egypt, one might ask? Isis was a goddess of ancient Egypt
depicted veiled; her statue at Sais bears the inscription : 'I am
mankind — past, present and to come. No mortal may lift my veil'.
   In ancient Egypt 'mortals' were those uninitiated in the
sacred mysteries. At one time in the distant past, initiates had
imagined Isis as giving birth to Horus, son of Osiris, but later
when Osiris had been killed by Typhon, god of darkness, the
initiates saw Isis incapable of giving birth and called themselves 'children of the widow'. (In an era of complete degeneracy
the priests called themselves 'the immortals' to distinguish
themselves from the uninitiated, a description later adopted
by French academicians).
   It is difficult to say whether Soloviev knew all this before his
visions but he represented her in just this form during his third
vision:

What is, what was, and what has yet to be,
All encompassed in one steady gaze

I saw all and all was one
One alone in the image of female beauty
The immeasurable within its measure
Thou alone, before me, in me.

Mark these words. Soloviev does not remark that 'No mortal may lift my veil'; his 'steady gaze' encompassed all past, present and future. The time has come when mankind must not hold back from spiritual questions, but on the contrary should put questions and demand answers from the spiritual world, as did Soloviev.

[The macrocosmic aspect of 'Sophia' coincides with the World Soul of Plato, the mysterious origin of human thought. In occult science this is called ' the aether of sounds' (Klang-aether) or the Pythagorean 'Harmony of the Spheres' which gives form to the Divine Word and enables it to sound throughout the cosmos. The World Soul is the spiritual atmosphere in which purified souls may breathe, 'live, move and exist' (Acts 17, 28). This divine atmosphere can be imagined as a canopy or baldachin sheltering these souls (as depicted by some artists), or in the form of the chalice of the Grail, a vessel encompassing all.]

The coming period of the 'Virgin Sophia' — or the purified souls — will belong to the spirit of the Russian people, if it follows the right path, the way of Vladimir Soloviev through the development of the spiritual aspect of the soul. Soloviev's experience of Sophia was the beginning of this development.

The poet Christian Morgenstern experienced Her as the Chalice of the Grail (I say 'Her' because I believe 'Her' to be the same as the Grail) and dedicated to Her the following verses: [14]

> To Thee I raise my heart aloft
> As the true cup of the Grail
> All my blood in thirst is spent
> For Thy holy nourishment
>   O Christ!
>
> Fill it to the brim again
> With Thy rose red blood
> That I may speak the news abroad
> Through earthly nights and days.
>   Thou art!

14 Christian Morgenstern, *Sämtliche Dichtungen*, I, Band II, Basel 1980, p. 61.

Ich hebe Dir mein Herz empor
als rechte Gralesschale,
das all sein Blut im Durst verlor
nach Deinem reinen Mahle,
    O CHRIST!

O füll es neu bis an den Rand
mit Deines Blutes Rosenbrand
dass: Den fortan ich trage
durch Erdennächt und -tage,
    DU bist!

In Russia there were people who dared to pose such questions and thanks to them some questions could already be answered by the start of the twentieth century. Dostoyevsky, Fedorov and Soloviev were such people. Already in his lifetime Soloviev obtained a whole series of answers to his questions; and later I shall mention how he anticipated various problems which were more fully dealt with by Rudolf Steiner.

Having hastened to respond to the call to Egypt which he later recognized as coming from Sophia, perceiving Her full stature under the starry vault of an Egyptian night, Soloviev thereafter devoted all his life to Her service.

Initially, and for some appreciable time thereafter, Soloviev regarded the manifestation of Sophia in this world as that Christians, both Orthodox and Catholic, called the Bride of Christ and holy protectress of all Christians, and what Russians in antiquity called 'Sophia the Divine Wisdom'. He had known her earlier; not for nothing had he studied philosophy and theology. To be a philosopher for him always meant to love Sophia (in the literal meaning of the word 'philosophy').

The true nature of Sophia is difficult, if not impossible, to explain logically. Spiritual experience can only be explained by a very accomplished initiate. Soloviev decided to relate his own experiences in this connection shortly before his death, in the 'stumbling rhyme' of his poem, as he put it.

Rudolf Steiner spoke of Sophia in the lectures on the Gospel of St. John.[13] The Virgin Sophia is part of the human soul, as yet

13   *Gospel according to St. John*, given at Hamburg, 18-21 May 1908 G.A. 103. However, this is not a quotation but a condensed summary of the content, as will be apparent.

developed only in very few individuals, but which will spread widely
in the cultural epoch following ours [during future millennia].
Sophia is the purified element of the developed soul, completely
liberated from all false egoism and all impurity; a soul capable of
bearing God's word within itself — 'Christ in you', as Paul puts it.

The closeness of these two poets, Soloviev and Morgenstern
is amazing. They relate to each other like sunrise to sunset —
Soloviev died at the very end of Kali Yuga* and carried with him
into the spiritual world those questions which for many prepared
the way to Anthroposophy, the Sophia in man.

[Rudolf Steiner spoke very often about Sophia without always
quoting her name, for example when he spoke of 'Goddess
Nature', a subject for Brunetto Latini (Dante's teacher), or of Isis
as experienced by the ancient Egyptians. The common identity of
these names becomes evident in the course of his lectures given
at Christmas 1920, when he stated the need for the creation of a
'new Isis legend':

> At the time when the Mystery of Golgotha was fulfilled,
> the divine Sophia, the Wisdom penetrating the world and
> enabling man to comprehend the world, was manifested in
> two ways: through the revelation to the poor shepherds in
> the field; and through the revelation to the Magi from the
> East. This divine Wisdom had been known among the
> Gnostics, whence it was taken up by the early Fathers and
> teachers of the Christian Church, who used it to understand
> the Mystery of Golgotha. But this Wisdom could not be
> transplanted into later times. It was overwhelmed, killed by
> Lucifer as Osiris had been killed by Ahriman-Typhon. What
> we today have lost is not Osiris, not Christ; what we have
> lost is the figure in the place of Isis. Lucifer has killed her.
> [That is to say that 'in our world-view ... the stars of heaven
> move according to purely mechanistic, amoral laws ... This
> is a purely Luciferic world-view.'] It is not as in the myth,
> where Typhon cast Osiris into the Nile and interred his
> remains. Rather Isis, the divine Wisdom, has been driven
> out into cosmic space, has been cast into the cosmic ocean.
> And in that we gaze into this 'ocean' of space, and see the
> relationships of the stars only in mathematical terms, the

---

* The 'Dark Age' said to have ended in 1899.

divine Wisdom is actually interred there — the spiritual principle which permeates the world, the successor of the ancient Isis, has been killed.

This legend is one we must undertake to create, since it embodies the truth of our times. Armed with a power which is within us, even though we do not understand it, the power of Christ, the new Osiris, we must set out and seek for the body of today's Isis, the body of the divine Sophia. We must approach the realm of Lucifer's abstract knowledge and seek there the grave of Isis ... She was not dismembered by Lucifer, as Typhon had dismembered Osiris. On the contrary, Isis in her true form is spread out, in all her beauty, over the entire universe. She confronts us in the manifold spectrum of colours, an aura of light coming from the entire universe. But just as Typhon had come to dismember Osiris, so now Lucifer has come to blur and confound these cosmic colours which make up the limbs of the new Isis, to fuse them into one undifferentiated white light: such is the nature of Lucifer.

We must understand that with the power of Christ we have to create an 'internalized' astronomy that can reveal once more how the cosmos is spiritually operative and works upon us. Thus we will have found once again the power of Isis, who has now become the divine Sophia; and Christ, who since the Mystery of Golgotha has been united with life on earth, will attain to his true reality within mankind because he can now be truly understood. It is not Christ that we lack, my dear friends! What we are lacking is the real knowledge, the Sophia, of Christ. [15]

Then at Christmas in 1920 Rudolf Steiner summarized these lectures (in which he referred many times more to the divine Sophia) in a meditation:

Isis-Sophia
Wisdom of God.
Lucifer has slain her,
And on his wings of temporal power

15   R. Steiner, *The Search for the New Isis — the Divine Sophia*, Spring Valley 1983.

Hence into cosmic space has carried her.
Christ's will,
At work in man,
From Lucifer shall wrest her
And through knowledge — spirit's soaring sails —
Restore to life in all men's souls
Isis-Sophia
Wisdom of God. 16]

For Soloviev philosophy was a weapon to use in the battle for Sophia. Alexander Blok named him a 'knightly monk' and said that Soloviev used philosophy as a knight would use his sword. Some present-day philosophers do not even know about Sophia; they play with thoughts as they might play at chess. Soloviev also very much liked playing chess, but his service to Sophia was for him no game. Today, if anyone knows about Sophia then they are probably poets, just as Goethe knew Her, and Novalis, Dante Soloviev, Bely and to some extent Blok and Morgenstern. There is no approach to Her through intellect.

With great perception Blok noted that Soloviev used intellect as a knight would use his sword, always behaving chivalrously; in his responses to thoughts, from whatever source, analyzing them often even more intelligently than had their author. Patience only failed him when he was in dispute with someone not objective or crudely biased. So it was in his polemic with Rozanov,17 one of the few original thinkers whom he met, and where the subject of dispute was the freedom of faith, a subject on which Soloviev easily lost his patience. Nevertheless, after the dispute he always tried to make peace with his opponent if he had taken umbrage, as he made his peace with Rozanov.

Soloviev gave himself completely to philosophy, looking upon it as a chivalrous weapon. He always saw the point of view of others in the most favourable light and invariably showed that a one-sided approach could lead to the abyss rather than to Superunity (a word introduced into the Russian language by Soloviev, and meaning, in essence, truth, Christ). In philosophy he always worked towards synthesis. His arguments

16 Rudolf Steiner, *Wahrspruchsworte*, Dornach 1925. Also G. A. 40.
17 *Works*, Vol. VI, p. 429 — Article by Soloviev 'Porfiry Golovlev on Freedom and Faith'; also Vol. IX, p. 278.

and polemics were mostly carried on in his articles in various journals. [Synthesis, Superunity (lit. 'All-one-ness') — these ideas are repeated continually in Soloviev's efforts to achieve unification of the Church of Christ or Christian oecumenicity after his return from Egypt. The battle for Sophia or Superunity explains his polemic against nationalism wherever it appeared. To separate one's own nation from the rest of the world and to make it into some sort of god appeared to him to be a sin against the unity of mankind, a sin against the spirit of Sophia.]

From early youth he began to fight with his best friends — Slavophiles, because he was already noticing in them some inclination towards nationalism, or as he put it, national selfishness. Starting with Yu. Samarin Khomyakov and A. N. Aksakov he finished with Katkov and Pobedonostzev, the most reactionary adviser of the Tsar, although the last-named he never specifically mentioned in print.

Although the first Slavophiles were liberals who potentially had a feeling for Sophia through the Church, [just as they were able to discern the cast of humanity generally in the ordinary people and something naive and unspoilt in the original Christianity of the Russian Church] it was clear that their tendency to consider the Russian Orthodox Church as superior to all others just because it was Russian, was not to Soloviev's liking, and in fact the Slavophiles moved from their slight nationalistic inclinations to intolerance and xenophobia and a hatred of Jews, Poles and even Old Believers and others. In this Soloviev proved a prophet.

In the article 'Love for the people and the Russian folk ideal'[18] included in the first edition of the book *The National Question in Russia*, Soloviev wrote: 'Usually, people wishing to extol their nationality use terms that themselves express the national ideal — whatever it is that they think is best and most desirable. Thus the Frenchman speaks of *beautiful* France and of French *glory* (la belle France; la gloire du nom français); the Englishman speaks lovingly of Old England; the German reaches higher and attributes an ethical character to the national ideal,

---

18 *Works,* Vol. V, p. 55, 1st Edition. 'Love for the people and the Russian popular ideal'.

proudly speaking of German faithfulness (deutsche Treue). In similar circumstances what does the Russian say in praise of Russia? Does he call it beautiful or old, or praise Russian glory or honesty? As you know, nothing of the sort is said; the Russian wishing to express the most profound feeling for his homeland speaks only of "Holy Russia" '. [In this ideal of the Russian people Soloviev also saw an underlying experience of Sophia. In that this ideal presupposes an element of the divine, Soloviev discerned its reference to the future : as if it were above the nation, not part of it, but an augury for the future.]

He did not write any articles in the journals directed against materialists and rationalists, because in the Russia of that time they could not have replied, and to attack someone who could not offer a defence he considered not only shameful but pointless.

Observing rules of chivalrous conduct in his support and service for Sophia, Soloviev never attacked Tolstoy, whose religious books were being published abroad. Not only did he watch his own conduct in this respect; he also warned others to guard against any such blatant lack of discretion, even by mistake, towards himself. Here is an extract from a letter of his to Kireyev, who, apparently unaware that everything written by Soloviev was proscribed by the Censor, had an article printed inveighing against Soloviev: 'In the circumstances your polemical article was a mistake which you must put right in so much as you can. We are old friends, and this old friendship, in my opinion, not only excuses my frankness on this issue, but obliges me to be frank' (1887).[19] Kireyev did not try to evade this injunction and attempted in vain to alter the decision of the Censor banning the publication of Soloviev's books. In purely philosophical books, however, he demolished materialistic ideas and was often sarcastic about them. [Serving Sophia was something which at that time was unprecedented. As one can ascertain, the conception of a cosmic soul did not exist then. None who were carelessly and thoughtlessly thinking about and energetically preparing for the catastrophe which overcame them in 1917, asked about the source of their thought. So Soloviev had to guard himself on all sides.]

19 *Letters*, Vol. II, p. 129.

Throughout his life Soloviev was forced to fight on two or even three fronts. In the Russia of those days power was in conservative hands while in society it was the materialists who were dominant. The Sophia of Soloviev's ideal was opposed to both, no less to inhuman reaction than to blinkered 'progress' and the inhumanity to which both would lead, which he foresaw and which we experience today. Soloviev defined his position thus:

> Poor child! Between the two enemy camps
> No refuge to be found. [20]

20 *Poems*, p. 75

Chapter Four

THE UNIFICATION OF CHRISTENDOM

Soloviev well understood that the dismembered institution, each part calling itself a differently named Church, could never embrace Sophia. For that the Church would have to be whole and undefiled. From 1883 he worked for the unification of the Church, and in this, as always, he was prepared to start with himself and his own Church, ready to make any sacrifice, ready to go to any lengths in order to create a true Temple of Sophia. [In essence Soloviev strove for the spiritual unification of Christianity, based on tolerance and acceptance of the opinions and conventions of others, even if these failed to correspond or even conflicted with his own feeling, as for example, in the matter of the infallibility of the Pope; his tolerance was based on the recognition that it is not in these things that the true essence of Christianity resides. He was prepared to abstain from argument deriving from the unenlightened exaggeration of human thought — dogma, which, after all, is not the most important thing in the world.]

Priest's blood ran in Soloviev's veins; he profoundly felt himself to be a member of the Russian Orthodox Church and he was never more at ease than in the company of Russian Orthodox Christians (this may be why he failed to find friends abroad). But even so he was prepared to accept all Catholic dogmas, including the infallibility of the Pope, in the interests of unifying the Church. In my view, dogmas did not interest him at all [which would explain why he was easily able to put up with those who continued to revere such idols.]

In this period he came in close contact with Ratschki, a colleague of Strossmayer, Martynov, Pierling, d'Herbigny and other important personages concerned about the unification of the Church. All were Catholics (d'Herbigny and Martynov were even Jesuits), but for a long time Soloviev believed that they shared his aims.

In 1886 he took specific measures towards the unification of the Catholic and Orthodox churches — measures however which he visualised differently from the Catholics and which were also misunderstood by the Orthodox in Russia. Soloviev went to Croatia where he engaged in lengthy discussions with the famous Bishop Strossmayer.

Strossmayer, the notable Bishop of Djakovo in Croatia, was a prominent Catholic cleric and an enthusiastic South Slav nationalist. He was considered to be one of the main protagonists for the unification of the Churches of that time. The nationalistic desire to unite the South Slavs was his chief motive. [The South Slavs of the West — the Slovenes and the Croatians — were Catholics, while the East Slavs — the Serbs and Macedonians — were Orthodox. Strossmayer calculated that a unified church would bring about political reunification of the South Slavs. The declaration of the infallibility of the Pope in 1870 destroyed all Strossmayer's hopes; this dogma alienated all non-Catholics.] Early in 1888 Pierling proposed to Soloviev that he should write a summary of his views in French. In this connexion Soloviev visited Paris, where he associated with Catholics and even made friends with some Jesuits. The summary of his thoughts grew into a quite substantial book which was published in Paris in 1889, entitled *La Russie et l'Eglise Universelle*.

Strossmayer arranged an audience for Soloviev with Pope Leo XIII, which should have taken place in the spring of 1888, but never did. Strossmayer wrote an introduction for Soloviev to the Pope using the words: 'A pious soul, innocent and truly holy' *(Anima pia, candida e vere sancta)*, but when the Pope read Soloviev's proposals for the unification of the Churches he said that it was 'not a bad idea, but without a miracle — impracticable' *(Bella idea, ma fuor d'un miracolo è cosa impossibile)*.

Soloviev knew well that intimate relations with Catholics carried the risk that gossip and rumour might be spread that he had become a Catholic. Thus, when he went to Croatia to meet Professor Strossmayer he was at pains to ensure that no one should think that he had accepted or would accept Catholicism.

On the way back from Paris, probably in the spring of 1888, Soloviev again stopped in Zagreb to see Strossmayer, and from there returned to Russia. In all probability he declined the audience with the Pope because of the disillusionment with Strossmayer's ideas. The rationalism of the Jesuits, the South Slavonic and Pan-Slavonic nationalism of Strossmayer, and finally the Pope's irony — these three blows brought to an end Soloviev's sympathies for the Westerners. Disillusion with the Eastern Church was not long in following.

Soloviev had visited Croatia, and Paris later, with great hopes, but as soon as he arrived he understood the practically undisguised ulterior motives behind the attitudes of representatives of the Western Church to reunification (or more correctly) unification of the two churches. He grasped, I think, that his Catholic associates were motivated by political and nationalistic considerations which were absolutely foreign to him. He parted company with the Jesuits who advised him not to write about Sophia. In a word, as mentioned in his letters, he had encountered the negative side of 'Latinism'.

From the letters referred to below, written by Soloviev between 1883 and 1892 to ministers of the Church, to the press, to friends and acquaintances, one can see how he tried to refute rumours that he had become a Catholic. In order to scotch such rumours while he was associating closely with Catholics and Catholicism and attending services almost every day with Professor Strossmayer, Soloviev made a point of receiving Communion daily in an Orthodox Church, even going so far as to have this certified in writing.

This was the period when he was most ready to accept all the disputed dogmas (to which, in my opinion, in his heart he felt completely indifferent), even the infallibility of the Pope, and when, moreover, he had even affirmed as in a letter he wrote to Kireyev, 'that any censure or anathema, even from the Catholic point of view, is concerned only with those in error as a result of malice'. [21]

On 8 April 1886 [i.e. before his journey to Croatia] he wrote to the Russian Archimandrite Anthony Vadkovsky about an evening spent in the Theological Academy in St. Petersburg: 'Yesterday I felt myself to be in truly Christian company devoted to God's work above all; this encourages me and gives me hope, and for my part I can give you hope — *that I will never transfer to the Latin Church* (Soloviev's italics). I have never suggested any kind of formal external union (in the sense which Kireyev ascribes to me) first, because I do not believe that it is possible, second, because I do not consider it to be desirable ...

21 *Letters,* Vol. II, p. 124.

and because I consider that any personal change of religion is just as unnecessary as an external union and in a sense damaging. Naturally I cannot cast any stones at those who convert from conviction, whether mistaken or not'. [22] The letter closes with the words: 'These statements will, I take it, suffice for well meaning readers to contradict the systematic libels uttered probably with the intention of creating practical difficulties for me'.

On 29 November 1886 he wrote again to Vadkovsky: 'I returned from abroad, having become more closely and intimately acquainted with both the good and bad sides of the western Church and even more convinced of my view that for the unification of the Church superficial union and personal conversion would be unnecessary and even damaging. To the attempts at conversion directed at me personally, I responded first of all by going to confession and communion in the Orthodox Serbian Church in Zagreb at an unusual time before the local priest Father Ambrose. In general I returned to Russia, if one can say so, more Orthodox than before I left. But there, possibly to test my steadfastness, I suffered an unexpected setback. Firstly, the religious censors completely banned everything I had submitted for publication even though it had nothing whatever to do with the tempting subject of Church unification. And secondly, at the same time there were furious attacks and libels on me in various journals, especially in theological publications, in so many words representing me as an apostate and enemy of the Russian Orthodox Church. These slanderous accusations, if they remain unanswered, will make it impossible for me to continue my work now, or in the future. *Maybe this is what they want'*. [23]

After this Soloviev lost all hopes of achieving any genuine reintegration of the Christian church from within and consequently the prospect of realizing the wisdom of the Mother and Virgin Bride of Christ within a human organization. In later years Soloviev was less concerned with this question and turned to seek Her in nature, expressing himself in poetry. But occasionally he returned to the earlier theme. On 11 January 1887 he wrote to his friend N. N. Strakhov: 'In these three weeks I have

22 *Letters,* Vol. III, p. 187.
23 *Letters,* Vol. III, p. 189. (My italics, E.G.).

experienced or have begun to experience spiritual loneliness with all its pros and cons'. [24] With this letter he sent a poem which shows his feelings then not only about the Church but also about the ancient so-called 'Fathers' of the Church:

> Ah, far beyond the snowy Himalayas *
> My friend dwells,
> But here I am alone, my ears assailed
> By yelping curs. **
>
> And frenzied monks in cruel dispute
> Distract my gaze,
> And the way of life of consecrated rogues
> From age to age.
>
> But once doze off and to the plateau of Tibet
> My soul flies,
> And to all the priests, the Cyrils and Nestors, [25]
> My goodbyes.
>
> Alas, blissful dreams of all too short duration
> Suddenly dissolve,
> And again the question of predestination
> Troubles my soul.

 * Not to be taken literally (V.S.).

** To be taken more than literally, thinking not only of yard dogs, but also of the hounds of literary religious journals (V.S.).

24 *Letters*, Vol. 1, p. 25.

25 In AD 415 Bishop Cyril, Patriarch of Alexandria, incited the populace against the important mathematician and philosopher, the great Hypatia. The crowd lynched her and dragged her body round the city streets. Hypatia's 'crime' was her refusal to associate herself with the Christians of the city where cruelty and Christianity were one and the same thing. In AD 403 at the Council of Chalcedon Cyril had already played a part in the condemnation and subsequent exile of John Chrysostom, one of the greatest Christians of his time. Later, during the Council of Ephesus, Cyril arranged the trial and exile of Nestorius, which led to the so-called Nestorian Schism, obliging the Syrian, Persian and Indian Christians to go their own ways in isolation. Thus Soloviev mentions in this poem both a 'consecrated rogue' and his victim.

Nevertheless, as well as antediluvian monks I also have to deal with live ones, who are always running after me, apparently seeking to buy me at a low price, whereas I will not sell myself even for a high one'.

On 16 July 1888 he wrote to Getz: 'Vague rumours reach me about gossip in the Russian press that I have become a Catholic, etc. In fact I am now further away from such a step than ever before'. 26

In 1890, in an undated letter, Soloviev wrote to Fet: 'My Jesuit friends scold me greatly for free thinking, dreaming and mysticism'. 27

On 28 November 1892 Soloviev wrote to V. V. Rozanov: 'I am just as far from Latin narrow-mindedness as from Byzantine, Augsburg or Geneva narrow-mindedness. The religion of the Holy Spirit which I profess is wider and at the same time more determinate than all separate religions: it is neither the sum of them nor a part of them, just as a person is neither the sum nor a part of his various organs'. 28

Several years later, in 1879, Soloviev wrote to the editor of *The New Times*:

'I consider it necessary to repeat what I have already stated more than once since 1883. I have never suggested any kind of official external union with Rome (as Kireyev would have it) firstly, because I do not think it would be possible; secondly, because I deem it to be undesirable; and thirdly, because I have never received authority to discuss it from those concerned on either side'. 29

26 *Letters*, Vol. II, p. 157.
27 *Letters*, Vol. III, p. 121.
28 *Letters*, Vol. III, p. 44.
29 *Letters*, Vol. III, p. 193.

Chapter Five

POSTHUMOUS CALUMNY

In 1910, that is ten years after Soloviev's death, when many of his friends were also dead, a letter appeared in the press, signed by a Uniate priest N. Tolstoy, Princess Dolgorukaya and Dimitri Novsky proclaiming Soloviev's secret canonical adherence to the Catholic Church on 18 February (old calendar) 1896. Here is the text of that letter:

In view of the doubts repeatedly expressed in our own and in the foreign press as to whether the late philosopher and religious thinker Vladimir Sergeyevich Soloviev was canonically received into the Catholic Church, we, the undersigned, consider it our duty to record in print that we were eye-witnesses to the reception of Vladimir Soloviev into the Catholic Church by the ordained Greek Catholic priest Father Nikolay Alekseyevich Tolstoy on 18 February 1896 (old calendar) in the private chapel in Father Nikolay Tolstoy's apartment, in the Sobolev building in Vsevolzhskiy Alley in the Ostrozhenka quarter. After confession before Father Tolstoy, Vladimir Sergeyevich read in our presence the creed of the Tridentine Council in the old Slavonic language, and then took Holy Communion after a service of the Eastern Greek rite (with mention of our Most Holy Father, the Pope) conducted by Father Tolstoy. Apart from ourselves there was only one other person present at this memorable event — a Russian girl in domestic service with Father Tolstoy. Unfortunately her name and surname are now impossible to establish. Having now publicly testified to our witness, we consider that there should be no further doubt about this matter.

Signed : Father Nikolay Alekseyevich Tolstoy
Princess Olga Vasilievna Dolgorukaya
Dimitri Sergeyevich Novsky

This letter was printed in *The Russian Word* of 21 April 1910 (old calendar) and reprinted in Warsaw in issue No. 8 of the journal

Kitezh in December 1927. I have been unable to verify it myself but have quoted the letter from the book by K. Mochulsky. [30]

Soloviev's nephew, Father Michael Soloviev, Professor Frank, Mochulsky himself and a whole series of other so-called Orthodox writers, accepted this 'evidence' and tried, each in his way, to explain this most peculiar action of Soloviev, but nobody questioned the truth of the allegation.

Luckily there is a telegram, sent by Soloviev to Alexey Alekseyevich Lugovy (editor of the monthly literary magazine *Niva*) on 20 February 1896, i.e. two days after the reported episode, regarding the second part of an article on the poet Polonskiy [31] which Soloviev should have submitted: 'Have been ill all the time. Must postpone until April'. Thus we are asked to believe that while unwell (a cold apparently) Soloviev got up from bed and ran off to a Uniate priest, unknown to anyone (if he indeed ever existed, which is difficult to confirm from outside Russia), at a time of his life when he was further away than ever from Catholicism, and that he was accepted into the Catholic Church by a priest and before witnesses, never previously mentioned in his correspondence, nor by any of those who wrote about him during his lifetime or thereafter, and this after his numerous statements that he considered union to be harmful. He repeats this in a letter to the editor of *New Times* in May 1897 correcting A. A. Kireyev: 'At no time have I ever proposed an "external official union" with Rome, as A. A. Kireyev ascribes to me, firstly, because I consider it impossible; secondly, because I find it undesirable'. [32]

Is it possible that after all the formal statements he had made ever since 1886 Soloviev had completely changed his ideas, and that he undertook this most serious step in secret; that he did so without telling anybody — neither his friend Lapshin (who recorded that Soloviev had always declared that 'this rumour was not true'), nor his friend and teacher Ivantsov-Platonov, nor any of his other friends to whom he wrote that he was further away from the thought of conversion than ever before?

To admit the faintest possibility that this could be true would

30 K. Mochulsky, *Vladimir Soloviev, Life and Studies*, Paris 1951, p. 217.
31 *Letters*, Vol. II, p. 309.
32 *Letters*, Vol. III, p. 193.

be tantamount to suspecting, or rather accusing, Soloviev of quite unbelievable mendacity.

If I understand the thought purported to be conveyed in the 'testimony' of the witnesses of 1910, Soloviev is supposed to have converted to catholicism to save his soul (in secret!) — he who throughout his life had been ready to sacrifice his soul for his friends' benefit. All sorts of clever people — even Professor Frank and Mochulsky — have accepted this silly invention without demur; nobody has highlighted the absurdity of the story, nor has anybody accused 'Father N. Tolstoy' (if such ever existed) of lying.

[Naturally this impossible tale must have emanated from some source, even though the authors may be known under quite different names. Obviously the source must have been Catholics anxious to appropriate the 'late philosopher and religious thinker' whose fame was growing from year to year, by means of a 'pious lie'. They have been most successful in their efforts; every book on Soloviev and nearly every encyclopedia relates the story unreservedly as a piece of most important information.

It appears that Eugenia Gourvitch is the first author to have recognized the significance of the telegram of 20 February 1896, clearly proving the impossibility of the so-called 'testimony'. Professor Frank, the Russian religious philosopher, who as an emigrant read lectures in Oxford, took great pains to 'explain' Soloviev's 'conversion', using various hypothetical speculations for his purpose, but apparently he overlooked that telegram which is included among Soloviev's letters. [33]

The so-called Uniate Church combines the Eastern liturgy in the appropriate vernacular language with the Western *filioque* dogma, and recognises the Pope of Rome as Head of the Church.(The *filioque* dogma says that the Holy Ghost proceeds not only from God the Father but 'also from the Son' — *filioque*.) It is important to remember that this church was actually banned in the Russian provinces of the Empire before 1917. That is why in 1896 and indeed in 1910 a Uniate priest could function in

33 A *Soloviev Anthology* arranged by S.L. Frank, London 1950, p. 25 and p. 249. Incidentally, Professor Frank quotes all relevant dates according to the new calendar, thus dating the 'conversion' 3 February. Here all dates are according to the original sources quoted, i.e. according to the old calendar.

Moscow only clandestinely and arrange Mass only in a private chapel in his own flat, as the 'testimony' says. However, it follows also that even in 1910 it would have been virtually impossible to prove or disprove the existence of the illegal Uniate priest N. A. Tolstoy. The Roman Catholic Church on the contrary was not forbidden in Russia and whether conversion had taken place or not could have been easily ascertained by reference to Church records. This is one of the points to be considered in evaluating the truth of the 'testimony'.

For an explanation of Soloviev's 'action' both Mochulsky and Frank rely to a great extent on a letter which he is supposed to have written in French to the French Catholic Eugene Tavernier in May 1896. Frank saw this letter as the key to the true meaning of Soloviev accepting communion in a Catholic Church in February 1896, i.e. about the same time as the letter. The letter is lengthy but the gist of it is as follows:

> These facts are certain and testified by the Word of God:
> 1. The New Testament will be preached throughout the earth, i.e. truth will be available to all people of all nations.
> 2. The Son of Man will find little faith on earth, i.e. true believers will form a numerically unimportant minority; the majority of mankind will follow the Antichrist.
>
> However, after a short and bitter struggle the party of evil will be vanquished and the minority of true believers shall be triumphant ... It is essential that: 1. A general system of Christian philosophy be developed since without it the acceptance of the New Testament cannot become effective. 2. If it is certain that in the event the Truth shall be accepted only by a minority suffering persecution in some degree, one must abandon the idea of the power and external greatness of Theocracy as direct and immediate targets of Christian policy ... 3. The certainty of the eventual triumph of the minority of true believers must not lead to an 'Altstück' of passive expectation. (Victory will not come as a sudden miracle). True believers form and will remain only a minority, and therefore they must attain qualitative and intrinsic strength, and the first prerequisite is a moral and religious unity — not arbitrarily established, but founded on a legitimate and traditional base, an obligation imposed

by piety. And since in the Christian world there is only one legitimate and traditional centre of unity it follows that true believers must rally round it which is all the more acceptable as it no longer possesses any external powers of compulsion. Accordingly each and every one may rally to it in the measure indicated by the individual's conscience.

On the face of it this letter could explain the secret conversion story. However, since the telegram of 20 February 1896 is clear evidence that the conversion testimony is false, doubts arise about Tavernier's letter and one must be permitted to investigate whether it is genuine or a fake.

To begin with the letter is not included in the collection of letters published between 1908 and 1911. It made its first appearance in 1916 in the introduction to Tavernier's French translation of Soloviev's *Antichrist* in Paris. It is printed in French and there is a Russian translation in the 1923 volume of *Letters*. Professor Radlov, editor both of this and the earlier volumes, obviously reprinted the letter from the book by Tavernier, and in the then prevailing political circumstances he was certainly unable to test it for authenticity. Professor Frank was right in thinking that the 'letter' would explain the 'action', but if the testimony is a lie, may the 'letter' itself not be a fake concocted to support the earlier falsehood?

The doubts about the authenticity of the 'letter' arise from an analysis of its contents and syntax. Superficially it seems that the 'ideas' contained in the letter are identical with those expressed by Soloviev in his *Antichrist*. Closer consideration inevitably leads one to the conclusion that the *Antichrist* ideas have been deformed and biased towards Catholicism. This is particularly pronounced in the following sentences in the letter (all underlining, punctuation etc. in brackets are by the editor):

'If it is certain that <u>in the event</u> the Truth shall be accepted (an event in the distant future) ... the true believers <u>are</u> ... a minority (present) ... they <u>must</u> attain ... and the first prerequisite <u>is</u> a moral and religious unity ... founded on a legitimate (?) and traditional (?) base. An obligation imposed by piety(?). And since in the Christian World there is (?) only one legitimate (?) and traditional centre of unity (?)

it follows that all true believers must (?) rally round it which is all the more acceptable (immediate future referring to present) as it no longer possesses (present) any external powers of compulsion and that accordingly each and everyone may rally to it ... '.

It is noticeable how cleverly whoever wrote the text of this letter mixes up far distant future, immediate present and immediate future, using only non-existent and imagined future conditions as reasons for immediate action and advice. The imagined future lack of power of an imagined future pope who remains true to the spiritual Christ is applied to the actual present 'centre' in Rome arbitrarily described as a powerless 'centre of unity'. A similar juggling act is performed with the words 'must' and 'may'. These manipulations are further supported by the inclusion of minor falsehoods supporting the argument. For instance, the require-ment of intrinsic, i.e. internal, strength demands a unity based on a legitimate and traditional, i.e. external, foundation, and this becomes an obligation imposed by piety. Similarly unfounded is the claim that in the Christian World there is a legitimate and traditional centre of unity — and that there is only one such centre — and that therefore all true believers must etc. It is indicative that whilst the centre is clearly described, it remains unnamed! Such juggling with words and conceptions so evident in the Tavernier letter is often considered to be typically Jesuitical. It is fairer to ascribe it to proselytising zealots among Catholics who are surely welcome neither to Jesuits nor to the Vatican.

As regards the superficial similarity of views expressed in the letter with those in Soloviev's *Antichrist*, the whole point of the *Antichrist* is that according to Soloviev there is only one centre of unity for truly believing Christians and that is 'Christ himself who is most dear to us and from Whom all derives'. (See below p. 98). All these political claims about legitimacy and tradition just disappear into thin air when faced with this confession of true belief. And so does the claim that Soloviev is supposed to have written this 'letter'.

To summarize: The Tavernier letter is without any evidence of authenticity and is likely to be a fake produced in 1916 to support the falsehood contained in the 'testimony' of 1910. In fact, the telegram of 20 February 1896 robs both 'Catholic' documents of all verisimilitude. One can only further add that the spirit and the contents of the 'letter' indicate quite a different source of authorship from that of the *Story of Antichrist.*

In her manuscript Eugenia Gourvitch simply ignored the Tavernier letter which naturally she knew well, apparently because she did not believe it worthy of consideration in view of the telegram the importance of which in this context she had discovered. It has been thought necessary to refer to the letter here is some detail in order to avoid possible misunderstandings.

Shortly before her death, Eugenia Gourvitch discussed the matter of the telegram and the letters with Paul M. Allen in a telephone conversation drawing his attention to the evidence. (I owe this information to Mary Trueman, Eugenia's faithful assistant, who witnessed the conversation.) In his recent book on Soloviev [34], Mr. Allen first repeated the conversion story and the usual attempts to explain it, but then in a supplementary chapter 'Regarding Soloviev's Conversion' referred to the new evidence, leading to the conclusion that the story of Soloviev's conversion can no longer be maintained. His work is thus, as far as we can see, the first published word of truth signalling the injustice done to Soloviev after his death.]

In the period following the date of his supposed conversion there is at least one important letter proving the absurdity of the 'testimony'. On 14 May 1897, i.e. about one year later, he wrote to the editor of *Novoye Vremie*, as he had already written on 8 April 1886 to Archimandrite Anthony Vadkovsky: 'A formal union with Rome, as Kireyev ascribes to me, I have never advocated, first because I consider it unattainable, secondly because I do not consider it desirable, and thirdly because neither side has authorized me to carry on negotiations to that effect.'

To accept the allegation as true would mean that Soloviev perfidiously and secretly betrayed the Russian Orthodox Church, and a year later betrayed himself in the press — in both cases without the slightest cause.

Soloviev first spoke of his relationship towards the reality of the earthly Catholic Church in his remarkable address on Mickiewicz [35], the Polish poet and statesman, on 27 December

34   Paul M. Allen, *Vladimir Soloviev, Russian Mystic*, Blauvelt, New York 1978, p. 283 and p. 411.
35   *Works.* Vol. IX, p. 257.

1898. In it Soloviev spoke of the three temptations of Mickiewicz and of his victory over these. The first temptation was his love for a woman, which resulted in unhappiness because another found preference before him. The second temptation was his love for his country, then torn to pieces and defeated by enemies, and the third was his love for: 'a supranational elect of an oecumenical Church, both historically based and transcending history'.

'But would it be a good thing on our part', continued Soloviev:

to treat such a consistory as an intellectual salve, conducive to laziness of mind and will and a dulling of conscience? How could we accept it on such a poor foundation? *And might not the consistory be infiltrated by those whose interest lies in our minds being atrophied and our conscience silenced?* No. In this world our human spirit can never and must never be at peace. No. There cannot and *must not be any authority to replace our reason and conscience* and make free investigation unnecessary.

The Church, like our native land, and like the biblical 'young bride', must be for us an internal force of tireless movement towards the eternal goal, and not a cushion of complacency. I reproach neither the tired nor the indolent, but in a discourse in memory of a great man it must be said that spiritual weariness is not a characteristic of great men.

Here let us not forget that spiritual weariness and indolence have two mutually supportive forms: on the one hand — being content with blind devotion to some external authority; on the other — being content to express slight disapproval. Some, so as not to trouble mind and will, are content with their own pocket-sized domestic idea of patent truth, while others, with the same aim of spiritual comfort, reject in advance, as an incongruous fiction, any task which is not immediately easy and comprehensible for them.

Both the former and the latter — those of lazy faith, and those of lazy doubt — find a common deadly enemy in what they call mysticism. And Mickiewicz has been condemned by both sides, as a mystic, especially because of the movement started among Polish emigrant society by Andrew Tovyansky.

These words could almost apply to Soloviev himself. Had not he also been deeply in love with a woman, loved his country and tried to liberate it from sin and falsehood, loved universal truth even more than his country and only late in life recognized the true nature of those who would not forgive him for his mysticism, and whose background of lies and selfishness he then perceived?

In a lecture in Moscow to the Psychological Society on 19th October 1891 Soloviev expressed a thought which up to then he had never put into words. This thought, completely misunderstood, but even in this form speedily reaching a wide public, put him in a very difficult position. Yet this lecture showed his capacity for uninhibited and daring expression not only as a free thinker but also as a clairvoyant.

In his speech he said that the disciples of Christ, that is the apostles, failed to understand Him at all during His life and only after His death on the Cross, on the day described as Pentecost, did they begin to understand Him whom they had been seeing every day. This is what he said:

The conversion and regeneration of even a single individual does not happen suddenly. Let us take Christ's own disciples. If anyone could, they possessed all the prerequisites for complete and speedy spiritual regeneration. However, throughout the life on earth of the Saviour and until Pentecost we note no such regeneration. They remained the same as they had been. The appearance of Christ amazed them. His spiritual power attracted and bound them to Him but did not transform them. They believed in Him as in a manifestation of a higher order and waited for Him to establish the Kingdom of Heaven, as an *external manifestation*.

And in them precisely, in these chosen people, in this salt of the earth, we can see the insignificance of this faith in the divine as an external supernatural manifestation. It is no accident, of course, that in the well-known Chapter 16 of St. Matthew we have side by side the highest praise for Peter for his fiery confession of the true faith, together with the denunciation of the same Peter: 'Get thee behind me, Satan: thou art an offence unto me: for thou savourest not the things that be of God, but those that be of man.'

It is not for nothing that the Gospel describes how this ardent disciple of Christ cut off the ear of the servant of the high priest in defence of his Master, and then that same night three times denied knowledge of Him. Only after external separation from Christ at His death were the disciples internally conquered and transformed by His spirit. Similarly He conquered the first community of the faithful in Jerusalem, said in the Acts of the Apostles to be of one heart and one spirit. But the Church in the widest sense, Christian humanity on the greatest scale, has never reached its Pentecost. [36]

From this alone can be seen how greatly Soloviev had altered his view that truth had been revealed in the Councils. And anyone who has the slightest knowledge of the proceedings of those Councils, and the assertion that the Holy Ghost inspired participants in the Councils, must feel that to say such a thing is to malign the Holy Ghost.

But in the real world one must have something stable to lean on. [This phrase has been repeated for nigh on fifteen hundred years and Soloviev was unable to abandon the point of view adopted by countless millions over so many centuries, supported with such assurance by all the churches. He had first to overcome it within himself.]

For a long time Soloviev justified to himself all the dogmas, even the infallibility of the Pope. [His tolerance here was the condescension used towards those who cannot be taken seriously.[37]] Nevertheless, even having gone so far, Soloviev could still not accept Catholicism. More important, a person of his character could never have done so secretly, concealing it from friends and public.

36   *Works*, Vol. IX, p. 381 — 'On the decline of medieval ideology'.
37   In a letter of 8 March 1900 to Mrs A. N. Schmidt he writes: 'The purpose of oecumenical Councils consists in finally formulating and announcing religious truths which have already been established, whereas that truth which concerns both of us still requires a lot of clarification'. *Letters 1923*, Vol. IV, p. 9.

Chapter Six

SOLOVIEV'S CHARACTER

In order to satisfy oneself as to whether Soloviev was capable of secretly adopting Catholicism simply in order to save his own soul, one need only appreciate to some extent the sort of person he was. In all truth, there have been very few saints on earth like Soloviev. There have been saints of the Christian Church as well as others certainly not belonging to it, even persecuted by the Church. There have been canonized saints such as St. Francis of Assisi; there have been those burnt at the stake by so-called 'churchmen' and later canonized, like the Maid of Orleans; there have of course been those of whom nothing is known, like the wild man described by Leskov in his story *At the End of the World*, but such people generally went off to monasteries or into the desert, followed by their disciples.

Soloviev lived in the world, in society, among professors, princes, ladies in waiting, students, nihilists, Jesuits, bishops, beggars and cabbies. (It is interesting that the Orthodox priest who heard Soloviev's confession as he was dying did not know him, whereas the cabbie who talked with the priest after the funeral did.) All without exception, including children and animals, sensed in Soloviev the enormous radiant power of his extraordinary individuality. Among his closest friends (closest in his opinion and in theirs) were Prince Tsertelev whom Soloviev greatly loved, although he asked him in conversation to leave 'God's people' (the Jews) alone as well as the Icon of the Mother of God of Czestohowo [38]; Prince Obolensky, meeting Soloviev after publication of one of his main philosophical books, asking him: 'Is it true you have written some sort of nonsense again?'; Countess Tolstoy, the wife of Aleksey Tolstoy (probably his only true friend); Countess Volkonsky, lady in waiting, who had accepted Catholicism despite Soloviev's advice; the poet Fet, an extreme reactionary; the poet Velichko; Kuzimin-Karavayev; V. V.

---

38 *Letters*, Vol. II, p. 259. Soloviev wrote a great deal about the Jewish question, e.g.: 'The Talmud and the latest polemic literature in Austria and Germany' (*Works*, Vol. VI, p. 3); 'The Jews, their religion and ethics' (*Works*, Vol. VI, p. 374), 'Jews and the Christian problem' (*Works*, Vol. IV, p. 142).

Rozanov; Leontiyev; Dostoyevsky; Professor Radlov, who later edited Soloviev's works and letters; the Jewish journalist Getz; the brothers Trubetzkoy, on whose estate he died, and many, many others.

Everybody loved him, but everywhere he was lonely and misunderstood. This was a strange destiny for one who opened his heart so widely to all, including even dogs and birds.

Soloviev was unusually handsome. Once seen, his looks were never forgotten. He was a remarkable speaker. Even Rozanov, whose eccentricity and taste for contradiction led him to say that he hated nobody more than Tolstoy and Soloviev, admitted that the latter could have appeared at a society reception dressed in a tailcoat and ginger trousers 'without ever losing his admirably aesthetic presence'. But despite all his charm, even the women who Soloviev loved most deeply and to whom he wrote such wonderful poetry, having perceived beyond them their higher egos, never returned his love and apparently found him difficult to get on with.

In his lectures on theocracy Soloviev expressed his social ideal. He said that according to the Old Testament people should be governed by a priest, a prophet and a king: 'The priest directs; the king manages; and the prophet corrects. Under this system of divine government, authority, based on tradition, belongs to the priesthood; the king has powers confirmed by law; while the prophet exercises free personal initiative.' [39] The achievement of the theocratic ideal requires the even development by agreement of these three instruments of divine government.

But Soloviev recognized that, apart possibly from the period of King David, this ideal had never been achieved on earth, because the Jewish people was by nature unsuited to monarchical government. It was not without reason that Samuel was so reluctant to agree to give them a king. But David was both prophet and king. His son Solomon introduced pagan cults into his kingdom, and it began to degenerate. Russia by its nature was adapted to the achievement of this ideal. Soloviev greatly loved St. Vladimir, who introduced Christianity to Russia.

Immediately after the assassination of Alexander II, in whose reign the peasants were freed from serfdom, Soloviev gave a lecture in the hall of the Credit Society in Moscow. As usual the hall was full and all the important personages of the time were present. Soloviev then spoke on these lines: [The text was never printed, but it must have been preserved somewhere, because Soloviev set out its content in a letter to the Tsar, Alexander III, although somewhat differently]:

Your Imperial Majesty, Gracious Emperor,

No doubt rumours in respect of an address I delivered on 28 March will have reached Your Majesty, probably in a distorted, but certainly in an exaggerated version. I therefore consider it my duty to report to Your Majesty exactly what I said. I believe that only the spiritual force of Christian truth can vanquish the powers of evil and destruction so prevalent today. I further believe that the Russian people in their entirety live and move in the spirit of Christ, and believing, finally, that the Russian Tsar is the representative and the expression of the people's spirit, repository of all the most benign national forces, I decided to testify to my belief to the public. At the end of my address I said the present difficult times give the Russian Tsar the unprecedented opportunity to proclaim the predominance of the Christian principle of forgiving all, thereby accomplishing a great act of morality, elevating his power to unassailable heights and confirming the unshakeable foundation of his rule. By pardoning those inimical to his power despite the natural instincts of the human heart and calculations and considerations of earthly wisdom the Tsar will rise to the level of the supernatural and thereby demonstrate the divine significance of his power. He will show that in him lives the supreme spiritual power of the entire Russian people, because in all this nation there is no man who could perform a greater deed. This is the substance of my address which to my great sorrow has been interpreted in a way directly contrary to my intentions.

I remain Your Imperial Majesty's obedient subject,

Vladimir Soloviev. [40]

40 *Letters 1923*, p. 149.

In the journal *Byloye*, printed abroad, the address was summarised thus: 'The father of the Tsar has been murdered. By ancient Old Testament laws his assassins should be executed, but in a Christian kingdom a different law should prevail, not "an eye for an eye", but "forgive your enemies". If the new monarch is Christian he will pardon his father's murderers; if not — he will show that he is something other than a Christian monarch and the Russian people will not tolerate a non-Christian Tsar, but overthrow him.'

Following this lecture Soloviev was hoisted shoulder-high by students of the left, but cursed by those on the right. To the remark of a minister that he could already smell Siberia, Soloviev replied that even in Siberia philosophy was possible. Having read Soloviev's letter the Tsar is said to have asked, 'Who is this Vladimir Soloviev?' On hearing that he was a philosopher the Tsar remarked, 'I knew he must be mad!'.

Soloviev was obliged to retire from his post [41] and everything he wrote from that time on was banned by the Censor.

Towards the end of his life Soloviev, thrown out of University because of his speech about the death penalty, denied by the Censor the right to publish his works, assumed editorial responsibilities for the philosophical section of the Encyclopaedic Dictionary of Brockhaus and Efron. He did not write on subjects connected with the dogma and history of the Church, which he knew so well. From all the Fathers of the Church he chose for himself his beloved Origen [42], considered half a heretic because of his belief in predestination, that is, in essence, reincarnation, which he understood from his studies of Plato. He also chose short notes on people like Hypatia, Martin of Tours, who believed in the salvation of the devil, which the Church regards as a heresy, and others especially significant in this context.

The short note about Hypatia is very interesting. The article on Cyril of Alexandria entitled *Cyril* was not written by Soloviev and deals with the instigation of the mob against Hypatia ascribed to Cyril of Alexandria and how the falsehood of this allegation has been proven by the Catholic writer Kopalik. But Soloviev in the

41 CM. *Works,* Vol. X, p. 13 — article by Radlov; the Minister, Baron Nicolay, is said to have remarked: 'I did not demand it'.

42 Brockhaus-Efron *Encyclopaedia,* Vol. 43, p. 140. Article on Hypatia: Vol. 16, p. 719; on Martin of Tours: Vol. 36, p. 696.

note on Hypatia does not mention this but says: 'She was brutally murdered by a fanatical mob incited by Cyril'.

In 1893 Soloviev wrote to the chief publisher of the *Encyclopaedia*, K. K. Arsenyev:

I am giving up the Gregory's for the following reasons. In the article about Gregory of Nazianzus (the theologian) I could not omit his views on the development of dogma, his opinion that the divinity of the Holy Spirit should remain a mystery because the general consciousness is still unprepared for this truth, and finally, his views that the Councils of bishops (in particular the second universal Council) were the greatest unmitigated evil for Christianity.

In an article about Gregory of Nyssa I would not be able to keep quiet about his denial of the eternity of suffering in hell, nor about his affirmation that the Holy Spirit derives also from the Son. If I were to write what I have indicated it would undoubtedly attract the attention of the Censor and might give P... (obviously Pobedonostzev) the pretext he wants for excluding me from the *Encyclopaedia*, just as I have been expelled from the learned societies.

About the third Gregory (Nicephorus or the miracle-worker) I would have only two things to say, also awkward, namely that all his works have been lost, probably not by accident, but because as a true disciple of Origen he was from the latest point of view a heretic, while at the same time enjoying a great reputation among Christian people as a miracle worker. [43]

But Soloviev wrote long articles about many heretics, knowing of course how they had been treated by the 'Fathers of the Church'.

In his thinking, in his social impulses, in his political views, and, most importantly, in his personal life, Soloviev always and everywhere served Christ and 'Her', who creates God's word. He pawned his only fur coat to help the needy, he argued with Dr. Petrovsky, a friend, that he, Soloviev, need not eat more frequently than once every two days, so that others might thereby have food daily (cf. Dr. Petrovsky's reminiscences of Soloviev); he

43 *Letters*, Vol. II, p. 87.

made his famous speech against capital punishment in Russia and consequently had to resign his professorship.

Lastly, the greatest sacrifice for him, which nobody to my knowledge has so far appreciated, was his preparedness to sacrifice his adherence to the traditions of the Russian Church, to which his beloved grandfather, the priest Father Mikhail, had devoted his life of religious service, and where as a nine year old boy, Soloviev had first encountered his eternal friend.

Careful study of Soloviev's character reveals in him two personalities: Soloviev the philosopher; social activist; publicist; ardent, impatient, always striving towards the same objective — synthesis, as described earlier; and Soloviev the profound mystic; poet; infinitely quiet. The Russian writer Teush, whose work has unfortunately never been published, has said that Jewish prophets are poets, and that prophets are always poets and poets always prophets.

[The subsequent chapters deal with that 'other personality', Soloviev the poet and prophet. The author's assuredness that the silly story put out posthumously by Catholic zealots was a barefaced lie is based on her awareness of Soloviev's spiritual and moral qualities. In this second part of her work she moves beyond the frontiers of her task to study Soloviev in the context of man's greatest achievement — knowledge of oneself — and thus she recognises the impact of Soloviev the prophet and his role in the future. Such an investigation is being attempted here for the first time in literature concerned with Soloviev.]

Chapter Seven

THE ETERNAL FEMININE

It is surprising that many poets and literary critics consider Soloviev to be unimportant as a poet. In my opinion he stands among the greatest Russian poets. Poets such as A. Blok and Andrey Bely knew this too and were profoundly inspired by Soloviev. All his images are the purest poetry and his words prefacing the third edition of his poetry are the absolute truth. Very few poets could say of themselves: 'In the end everlasting beauty will bear fruit and bring about the salvation of the world, when illusion will fall away like the sea foam that gave birth to the primordial Aphrodite. My verses serve her by more than words, and that is the one inherent quality which I can and must claim for them'.

Soloviev's philosophy, great as it is, nevertheless has something impermanent about it, something dogmatic and intellectual. His poetry is free of this. The best and most important of his poems are dedicated to Her, as is the case with many other great poets. Dante, Goethe, Novalis, Morgenstern and Soloviev, all knew Her and wrote of Her. For Soloviev She manifested Herself in the gold and emerald fields of Egypt. He saw her everywhere as the inaccessible, eternal, veritable mystery of life on earth, the soul of the earth, from which in accordance with the ancient Isis legend, everything that is alive 'lives, lived and shall live'.

At the same time, despite his search for Sophia in Egypt, Soloviev clearly differentiated between his image of Sophia and his representation of the ancient Isis. He sought and found this mystery wherever earth 'lives'.

The Nile Delta

> Gold and emerald fields,
> Rich, black soil,
> Generous, silent
> Land of toil.

Fertile womb
Through centuries sleeping
Seed and corpses
Equally accepting.

Not all ye bear
Will rise again each year,
That pledged to age-old death
Awaits no spring.

Nor thrice crowned Isis
Will lead to that spring
But the 'Lady of the Rainbow Gates' *
Inviolate, eternal. 44

*   A Gnostic expression. V.S.

As a clairvoyant Soloviev was especially engrossed in the course of nature in the autumn. He knew that elementary spirits emerging from the earth in the spring returned there in the autumn, as described in his poem *The Autumn Road*.

He heard the message of the white bellflowers on Countess Tolstoy's estate which was so dear to him; bowed to the 'Earth-Sovereign' whose beating heart he felt; contemplated the gold and emerald fields of Egypt, as already remarked, and perceived Her beneath the snows of Finland. In his poetry Soloviev account for his past and present experience and expressed intentions for the future.

The Autumn Road

Dusk falls. Over a tired pale land
Clouds hang motionless.
The golden leaves of birth and linden
Shine in farewell dress.

The spirit is seized by sweet sad dreams
The infinite distances dim
And the reconciled soul feels no regret
For the bright and noisy spring.

44 *Poems*, p. 91.

As if the earth, retiring to its rest
In wordless prayer engages
And from the sky a silent unseen flock
Of pale winged spirits descends. [45]

White Bellflowers

'... and I heard a heart in flower'. — Fet

So many have been flowering recently
In the woods, like a white sea!
Warm breezes rocked them gently
Protecting their fragile beauty.

She is fading, she is fading,
Her snow-white garland yellows,
As if all the world were wilting.
I stand alone among their graves.

'We live on, your white thoughts
Along the soul's hidden pathways
Shining motionless and silent
While you trudge the gloomy highway.

The fickle winds do not protect us
But you we can protect from blizzard ...
Better come through the rainy west
And to you we will be — the cloudless south.

When mists your vision obscure,
Or threatening thunder sounds nigh —
Our heart will breathe and flower.
Draw close and find out why'.

15 August 1899 [46]

Soloviev also felt the beating pulse of Sophia in the Russian soil:

45 *Poems*, p. 91.
46 *Poems*, p. 185.

Earth — Sovereign! To thee I bow my head,
And through thy fragrant robe of earth
I sense the tremor of worldly life,
And feel the flame of my born heart.

In the warm voluptuousness of the noon sun
You descend to bless the radiant skies
And the free flowing river sings a greeting
In chorus with the forest's many voices.

And in this manifest sacrament I see again the meeting
Of supernatural world and earthly spirit
And by love's flame material suffering
Is scattered and dispersed like wisps of smoke. [47]

He found Her in the snows of Finland:

On Lake Saima

All wrapped about in fleecy fur
In quiet untroubled sleep Thou liest.
No death here in the brilliant air
And the clear white silence.

In this profound unruffled peace
I sought Thee not in vain
With insight seeing Thee the same
As the fairy queen of cliffs and pines.

Thou art chaste as the mountain snow,
Thoughtful as winter nights,
Brilliant child of dark chaos,
Radiant as the Northern Lights. [48]

47 *Poems*, p. 88.
48 *Poems*, p. 133.

Thinking of Her, while studying cabbalistic books:

And in my Queen's green garden
Bloom the fairest of lilies and roses,
And the clear surge of argent streams
Reflects Her brow and tresses.

But She neither hears the whispering streams
Nor sees the flowers' beauty.
Grief clouds Her sky-blue eyes
And Her thoughts are filled with sorrow.

For far away on the midnight edge
Midst freezing cloud and storm
She sees Her lost friend weaken
Fighting evil alone.

And She casts aside Her diamond crown
And quits Her golden halls
And stretches Her protective arms
Towards Her faithless friend.

Above the winter's gloom
A bright new spring extends
Its shining mantle to cover him
Peacefully, caressingly.

Dark forces vanquished below
He glows in the clear flame,
While to Her friend She quietly speaks
With eternal love in Her blue eyes:

'Your will is as fickle as the waves of the sea;
You swore to keep your faith to me,
And forswore that faith; but your treachery
Could hardly change my fidelity'. [49]

49 *Poems*, p. 63.

Listening to the songs of the Ophites or Snake Worshippers:

Song of the Ophites

The white lily and the rose
The red rose we combine
Our strange prophetic dreams
Reveal truth outside time.

Utter prophetic words!
Cast in the bowl thy pearl!
Let our dove be bound
With the age-old snake's new coils.

Why fear Prometheus' fire?
The free heart has no pain ...
In the great snake's fiery coils
The pure dove free remains.

All hail to violent storms
Peace there we shall find ...
The white lily and the rose
The red rose we combine. 50

Soloviev addresses 'a word of admonishment' to elemental
spirits — the sea devils, prophesying Her immediate return. (This
poem has a German title, after Goethe).

DAS EWIG — WEIBLICHE
(A word of admonishment to the sea devils)

The sea devils are after me
Snapping at my heels.
They were hot on the trail recently
In the Finnish isles.

50 *Poems*, p. 65.

Clearly they seek my demise,
As devils by their nature do.
God be with you devils
    but believe you me
I won't be devoured so easily.

Rather listen to what I have to say,
Kind words saved especially:
Whether you revert to being
        God's creatures
Depends, dear devils, on you.

Remember how by that sea
Where Amafunt and Pathos stood,
For the very first time in your lives
You suddenly felt ill at ease.

Remember the roses in the
        white spindrift,
The purple reflections in the
        azure waves,
Remember the figure of the
        beautiful body,
Your shame and trembling and fear.

Devils! By beauty's first defence
You were not long restrained.
She had no way of conquering
Your wild lust first subdued.

Crafty devils, you soon found
Secret access to her beauty,
Seeding in that splendid form
Devil's seeds of death and decay.

Know you then:
        the Eternal Feminine now
Comes to the earth in form inviolate.
In the radiant light of the new Goddess
Sky and rolling waters merge.

All that made lovely the earthly Aphrodite,
The joy of homes and woods and sea
All subsumed in supernatural beauty,
Stronger, more alive,
    all-encompassing purity.

Clever devils, you would seek in vain
To get at her, so why try?
She to whom all nature is in thrall
You cannot defeat or delay.
Proud devils, you are male all the same
And it is shameful to argue with a lady,
Dear devils, if only for that reason,
Give up and go away. [51]

White Bellflowers Again

Hot, thundery
Summer days
White, comely
The same ones again.

Ghosts of spring
Scorched maybe,
Strangers here,
Dreams of reality.

Malice forgotten
Cools in the blood;
The pure sun of love
Ascends instead.

Brave plans
In the hurt heart
Like white angels
Rise all around.

---

51 *Poems*, p. 163.

Ethereal, comely,
The same ones as ever
In the hot, heavy
Stifling weather. [52]

The question naturally arises why in his poetry Soloviev should mention the eternal feminine so often and Christ so seldom. In one of his last poems he writes 'The Eternal Feminine now / Comes to earth in form inviolate', but he says nothing anywhere of the resurrected Christ walking abroad eternally although he certainly felt this and wrote as much in his philosophical works, for instance in his dissertation on 'Godmanhood'.

To explain this I would like to return to the goddess Isis. Rudolf Steiner said in his lectures on the *Mysteries of the East and of Christianity* that Egyptian initiates saw Isis as aspiring to give birth to Horus although unable to do so. The initiate in these Mysteries was called 'a son of the widow' (as was Hiram, architect of Solomon's temple). However, Sophia was no such widow, but, as Soloviev says, using Gnostic terminology, 'The Lady of the Rainbow Gates'.

This is what Rudolf Steiner said of Sophia (it should be noted he spoke very little of Her, just as he said little of Jesus Christ until obliged to do so when Annie Besant announced the reincarnation of Christ as an Indian boy). In stating that Christ would not appear again in physical form, Steiner, in his series of lectures *The Gospel of St. John*, affirmed the Mother of Christ to be Sophia, that is the completely purified and enlightened spirit of the world, present at the crucifixion and given by Christ into the hands of his favourite — his devoted disciple John.

When man purifies his soul, and to the extent of that purification, his soul is transformed into the Sanskrit *Manas*, that is, into Sophia, becoming the microcosmic Mother of God — the spirit of the world. Soloviev came close to this conclusion in his poems 'Earth — Sovereign' and 'The Nile Delta'.

---

52 *Poems*, p. 100.

Chapter Eight

RUDOLF STEINER ON SOLOVIEV

[Since the dawn of the 20th century, and more specifically from 1910 onwards, Steiner expressed the view that mankind stood at the beginning of a decisive change in its spiritual constitution. Until the beginning and even until the second third of the century man's consciousness relied exclusively on his physical senses and the intellectual understanding connected with them. For a long time this will continue to be so for the majority of mankind, but now and from the second third of the century there will arise in a few individuals and then in more and more people a new conscious ability — besides the intellectual consciousness which they will keep to the full. It will be a 'new kind of clairvoyance' not suppressing intellectual understanding but endowing man with a completely new orientation towards nature and nature's forces and also towards the human and inner life.

Intellectual understanding was not originally man's normal state of consciousness. We can see this when studying works of the human spirit handed down to us from ancient times. In the Bible Adam, Abraham and Moses communicate with God as with their equal. This former consciousness — which many authors term 'the mythical consciousness' — was clairvoyance which however excluded the use of intellectual understanding. Understanding in the sense of the word began developing at the earliest some 5000 years ago, about the time when script was invented. The spiritual constitution of man continues developing, says Steiner, and since 1910 he gives greater precision to his view in prophetic prediction to the coming clairvoyance. In this context Steiner refers several times to Soloviev as a precursor of a consciousness where the intellect and the elevated consciousness do not exclude one another, but belong together — as sleeping and waking do not exclude one another, but fulfil two correlated tasks.]

In a lecture delivered in Locarno on 19th September 1911 Steiner probably speaks about Soloviev for the first time:

A long time will elapse before human beings learn how to see with the eyes of the spirit. But the faculty will arise in the twentieth century and in the course of three thousand years will be acquired by people in ever increasing numbers. The next three thousand years will be dedicated to the achievement of this goal. But in order that these things may come to pass, the main streams of evolution under spiritual guidance — are such that human beings will be able to acquire greater understanding of the principles of the occult life.

There are two main streams. The one may be recognised in Western thought, where we find that the most elementary and fundamental concepts of the spiritual world have sprung from the foundations of pure philosophy. Remarkable things come to light when we study what has happened in the cultural life of the West. We find people developing purely intellectually, and others practicing religious observance (and others who do both) their minds nevertheless also possessing the gift of the inner eye enabling them to look into the spiritual world. Everywhere we perceive a spiritual life which stems from Occidental philosophy. I will only refer to Vladimir Soloviev, the Russian philosopher and thinker, a seer in the real sense although direct vision of the spiritual world came to him only three times in his life. The first time was at the age of nine, the second time in the British Museum and the third time in the Egyptian desert with the stars above him. There broke in upon him then a revelation that could only be perceived with the eyes of clairvoyance, taking the form of prophetic vision of human evolution. [53]

On 9th February 1912 in the lecture 'Intimacies of Karma' given in Vienna Steiner says:

[53] All treatises and lectures of Rudolf Steiner are now available in the original German in the *Gesamtausgabe* and all references in footnotes refer to this complete edition. This lecture is published in G.A.130, p. 32. The translation here is based on D. S. Osmond's published in *Anthroposophical Quarterly*, 1968.

Those responsive to what takes place in the occult spiritual life of the world were confronted with a peculiar phenomenon. If you experienced in the eighties or nineties of the last century what was taking place around us on the spiritual plane you could feel occultly certain influences emanating from a remarkable personality ... but they were felt so as to make you somewhat uneasy in experiencing them. And all those who can feel influences from contemporaries very far away, felt at that time something radiant emanating from a certain personality which was not quite harmonious. Then, at the beginning of the new century one experienced that the influence had become harmonious. What had happened? I will now tell you the cause. On the 12th of August 1900 there died a personality who indeed has not been fully appreciated: it was Soloviev. He had an ether-body (life-body) of a radiant quality and it shone forth far and wide. But although Soloviev was a great philosopher, his head, his intellect, was not as far advanced as his soul. His thoughts are great and beautiful, but his conscious philosophy was not of the same value as what he bore within his soul. Until his death this was impaired by his head, and so you felt his occult influence as lacking in harmony. But when he died and his head-forces had separated from his ether-body, the ether-body continued to shine forth in the ether world, now rid of his thinking, no longer affected by it, and it shone forth and radiated in the most wonderful way. [54]

In the spring of 1912 visiting Helsinki he gave a series of lectures on *The Spiritual Beings in the Heavenly Bodies and in the Kingdoms of Nature*, and he also gave an additional address to his Russian listeners who had come to Finland to hear him. A year later, on 5th June 1913, on the occasion of another visit to Helsinki to lecture on *The Occult Significance of the Bhagavad Gita*, Steiner delivered another 'Address for Russian Listeners only'. (Originally Steiner had been invited by Russian friends to give the lectures in Russia, but the Russian Government refused permission to enter Russia). In these wonderful Addresses

[54] G.A. 130, p. 271.

Steiner describes the beauty of the young soul of the Russian people — the Archangel of the Russian people — and the astonishing future awaiting their Folksoul, destined to flourish in the sixth post-Atlantean cultural epoch if the Russian people will be worthy of it.

[These periods of civilization were defined by Steiner both empirically and astronomically; empirically by historic observation of the great world civilizations that take a little more than 2000 years to develop, evolve and decay. The creative centres of the Egyptian-Babylonian epoch for instance flourished in the third and second millennia BC, whilst the civilization determined by Greece and Rome took place essentially between a millennium BC and a millennium AD (naturally the after-effects work on into the following millennium). With regard to the first agricultural civilisation which originated in ancient Persia radioactive carbon tests have placed its main development in the fifth and fourth millennium BC.

These chronological empirical facts coincide, as Steiner points out, with the 12 subdivisions of Plato's astronomical 'Great Year'. The 'Great Year' comprising 25,920 solar years is due to the vernal equinox of the sun advancing a little every year. Every year spring equinox arrives a little earlier, only a little every year, but sufficient for it to arrive one month earlier every 2,160 solar years, an advance which can be ascertained by the sign of the Zodiac when the equinox comes. Two thousand years ago, during the Graeco-Roman epoch the sun at vernal equinox would be in the sign of Aries, whilst it is now in the sign of Pisces. During 25,920 years the sun travels all round the Zodiac. One twelfth of the duration of each of the great civilizations. According to this calculation the sixth post-Atlantean epoch would start in about 1600 years, when the vernal equinox point of the sun will enter the sign of Aquarius. The expression 'post-Atlantean' as used by Steiner coincides approximately with the usual prehistoric geological term of 'post-glacial age'.]

In his address to the Russian listeners of 11th April 1912 Steiner said:

The spirituality expressed in theosophy can be found by a soul thirsting for it, longing for it ... the Russian Folksoul — and this I know — is longing for the spirit which finds expression in theosophy. The Folksoul is longing for it with all the forces it is able to develop. Most tragically it appeared before my eyes ... around 1900. It then showed itself in a most tragic way, because then I noticed something which I could not explain to myself correctly until much later — it showed how in point of fact this Russian Folksoul is even today still meeting with very poor understanding. In Western Europe we have received much, very much that has come to us from Russia, and much that has come from Russia had made a deep impression on us who live to the west of Russia. We have become familiar with the great impulses of Tolstoy as well as with the deeply moving psychology of Dostoyevsky, and we have at last recognised a spirit such as Soloviev — a mind who will give you the impression that he and his writing are a whole, if you are open to his influence; and you will see in it the right light only if you sense the Russian Folksoul standing behind him. And this soul of the Russian people can express more, much more than even Soloviev is able to say, for there is still far too much that is accepted by Western Europe coming before our hearts.

Let me impress upon you, my dear friends, the word: responsibility. Remember that it is your task to show yourselves worthy of the Russian Folksoul and to realize that there is a longing in this soul for a theosophy purified of personal aspirations. If you come to know theosophy and its innermost impulse, then you will have to pose diverse questions — questions that can only be raised by the Russian Folksoul: questions of the soul to questions of the spirit in theosophy.

I have experienced so much of a noble, magnificent and beautiful feeling coming towards me from Eastern Europe, and so much of true and genuine love and goodness if subtle and intimate observation of what is in the world and of instances of intense and personal involvement with the powers that govern existence. And arising from such dear beautiful noble feelings a great many questions have been put to me by members of the Russian people — questions which indeed *must* be raised because mankind will not be able to exist in the future if these questions cannot be answered. Such questions can come only from the East of Europe. Up to now they have been put to me only by the Russian people's soul — the Folksoul in the higher worlds. I have often had occasion to think that the children of this Folksoul have still some way to go before they will come to understand their Folksoul, to understand what this Folksoul is really yearning for and how much still separates it from its children, the Russian people. Therefore do not shrink from seeking the way to your Folksoul — you will find it if you are determined to do so. From out of your people's Folksoul you will discover those questions that must be answered, for without them mankind of the future will no longer be able to exist. Do not recoil from the task of having to overcome all personal aspirations and remember this feeling of responsibility, for in the coming time the Folksoul of the peoples will stand in need of their children, the 'human beings'. [55]

In the series of lectures *From Symptom to Reality in Modern History* Steiner speaks again of the special relationship of Soloviev to the Russian people and to European culture as a whole.

[Steiner distinguishes here three characteristic attitudes existing in Europe 'since the beginning of the 15th century' towards the phenomenon of the continuing impulse deriving from the Founder of Christianity. The attitude centred in Eastern Europe, was prepared and effectuated in the 9th century by the conflict between Pope Nicholas I and the Patriarch of Constantinople, Photius, which led to the Great Schism separating the Western from the Eastern Church. This event had the effect of 'pushing back the Christ-Impulse' in its special intensity towards the East of Europe and led to the establishment of a 'true Christ-people', a metamorphosis of the Christ-Impulse where the inhabitants of this region kept their souls open for the ever-inflowing of the Christ-Impulse for the ever-living presence of the breath of Christ. And this special metamorphosis being pushed towards the East caused the Russian people to become the 'Christ-people' within the European civilization in the widest sense of the word.

55 G.A. 158, p. 203.

As opposed to this the second differentiation exists 'where the spiritual reign of Christ is transformed into a worldly reign of the Church, wherein at the same time the revelation of Christ becomes a question of worldly power and brings about a confusion of political power and ecclesiastical administration'. This fundamental different attitude towards the Christ-Impulse came from Rome and culminated in Jesuitism. And all those people who were influenced by Rome took on a special character, one could designate them 'People of the Church'. Within the actual people of the Church there exists however a spiritual entity which is diametrically opposed to Jesuitism — that other element which is reluctant to allow the spiritual to interfere directly with profane government structures. It wants to see the 'Christ-Impulse' influencing the souls and only indirectly through the souls influencing the outer world. Deriving from Goethe this approach is called 'Goetheanism'.

A third active influence among the European peoples had its roots originally in the Celtic culture areas. It is an anti-democratic and well organised aristocratic element *with* a certain strong tendency for living in a social community, but so that there were the rulers and the reigned over, leaders and the led. King Arthur and his Round Table appear as an imaginative prototype of this social ideal. This attitude led to an organizing of the social element and dealing with the spiritual as part of the social community.

In this way there arose in Western Europe and in particular in the English speaking countries something that one could call 'peoples of the Lodge'. With this third and most westerly attitude towards the Christ-Impulse the impulse itself became thoroughly questionable and still more stunted than with the people of the Church. In the end this led to so-called Deism, the philosophic conception of modern enlightenment. 'God created the world, but has withdrawn from it since'. Here Christ is brought down and converted into a Teacher, whereas for the people of the Church He is King and for the Christ-people Christ is the Spirit.]

In the lectures *From Symptom to Reality in Modern History* Steiner says:

What do we really mean when we speak of the Christ-people? It means that there was a territory created in

Eastern Europe where there were always human beings who were directly connected with the Christ-Impulse — human beings in whose souls in a certain way the Christ-Impulse exerts a continuous influence. Christ remains continuously present as a penetrating inner aura in the thinking and in the feeling of these people. Probably we could not find stronger evidence for what I have just said — and evidence it is indeed — than the personality of Soloviev, the greatest philosopher of the Russian people in recent times. Read him and feel how there is in him a direct inflow of what may be called 'Christ-inspiration' (notwithstanding certain traits in him on which I have commented in other contexts). Feel how the Christ-inspiration is working so forcefully in his soul as to make him conceive even the whole structure of external social life as regulated by the invisible Christ, by Christ the King of the human social community — that everything becomes permeated by Christ and every single action accomplished by man to be really performed by the Christ-Impulse active in Man right into the very moving of his muscles. Soloviev is the purest, the most beautiful representative of the Christ-people.

Steiner mentions Soloviev twice more in his lectures:

Soloviev wishes as it were to raise the worldly Kingdom to the heights of the divine Kingdom, but not to reduce the Kingdom of God to the depths of the Kingdom of the World.

It is the opposite (to Jesuitism) to endeavour to raise continuously what is down here to the level of the spiritual world rather than to bring down what is above, and such an approach is like a natural endowment of the Christ-people. Though hesitatingly it found expression in Soloviev. [56]

In 1924, in one of the last lectures which Rudolf Steiner was able to give, he spoke again of Soloviev. It is one of the so-called Karma Lectures of Steiner's. He discloses in them his insight into

56 *Esoterische Betrachtungen, karmischer Zusammenhänge,* G.A.
     238, p. 126.

concrete and individual connections of reincarnation. The rein-
carnations mentioned include those of personalities with whom
one is acquainted in external history. Before these lectures he
had hardly ever spoken about it because his listeners did not
seem to be ready to receive the message. Steiner insisted that the
contents of these lectures should never be conveyed in an
abridged or summarized form, but should always be quoted in
full. Just before speaking about Soloviev he says that he would
mention certain cases of individual incarnation and reincarnation as examples to demonstrate 'how important contemporary
personalities bring the past into our times'. He then continues:

> I will now take an example, which will probably be of great
> and deep value to you all. Though I almost shudder to
> speak of it in any easy way, yet I cannot but choose it, for it
> leads so infinitely deeply into the whole spiritual texture of
> the present time.
>   I will now mention another personality, of whom, as I
> said, I almost shudder to speak in this way. And yet he is
> infinitely characteristic of all that is carried from the past
> into the present and of the way in which this happens. I
> have often referred — and you will know about it from
> history textbooks — to the Council of Nicaea, which was
> held in the 4th century, where the decision was made for
> Western Europe as between Arianism and Athanasianism,
> and Arianism was condemned. It was a council in which the
> important personalities were imbued with all the high
> scholarship of the first Christian centuries, and brought it
> forth. They did indeed dispute with deep and far-reaching
> ideas. For in that time the human soul had still quite a
> different mood and constitution. It was as a matter of
> course for the human soul to live directly within the
> spiritual world. And they were well able to dispute with real
> content and meaning as to whether Christ was the Son, of
> the same essence with the Father, or only of like essence
> with the Father. The latter was the standpoint of Arianism.
> Today we will not go into the dogmatic differences of the
> question. We will only bear in mind that it was a question
> of immensely deep and sharp-witted controversies, which
> were, however, fought out with the peculiar intellectualism

of that time. If today we are clever and sharp-witted we are so as human beings. Indeed today, as I have often said, almost all men are clever. They are really dreadfully clever — that is to say, they can think. Is not that right? It is not saying much, but it is a fact that they can think: I may indeed be very stupid and still be able to think ... but it is a fact that the men of today can think. In those times it was not so. It was not that men could simply think, but they felt their thoughts as inspiration. He who was sharp-witted felt himself gifted by the grace of God, and his thinking was a kind of clairvoyance. It was still so in the fourth century AD, and those who listened to a thinker still had some feeling of the living evolution of his thought. Now there was present at the Council of Nicaea a certain personality who took an active part in these discussions, but at the end of the Council he was in a high degree disappointed and depressed. His main effort had been to bring forward the arguments for both sides. He brought forward weighty arguments for both Arianism and Athanasianism. And if things had gone as he wished, undoubtedly the result would have been quite different. Not a wretched compromise, but a kind of synthesis of Arianism and Athanasianism would have been the outcome. — One should not construct hypothetical history, but this may be said by way of explanation. — It would probably have been a very much more intimate way of relating the divine in the inner being of man to the divine in the universe. For, in the way in which Athanasianism afterwards evolved these things, the human soul was very largely separated from its divine origin. Indeed, it was thought heretical to speak of God in the inner being of man. If, on the other hand, Arianism alone had won the day, there would of course have been much talk of this God in the inner being of man. But it would not have been spoken of with the necessary depth of reverence, and above all, not with the necessary inward dignity. Arianism alone would indeed have come to regard man at every stage as an incarnation of the God who dwells within him. But the same may be said of any animal, indeed of the whole world, of every plant, of every stone. Such conception has real value only if it contains at the same time the active impulse to rise ever higher and higher in spiritual development, for then only do we find the God within. The statement that there is a divine within us at any and every stage of life can have meaning only if we take hold of this divine in a perpetual upward striving of the self by whom it is not yet attained. But a synthesis of the two conceptions would undoubtedly have been the outcome if the personality to whom I now refer had been able to gain any decisive influence at the Council of Nicaea. He failed. Deeply dissatisfied, he withdrew into a kind of Egyptian hermitage, lived a most ascetic life, and was deeply imbued at that time in the fifth century with all that was the real spiritual substance of Christianity during that age. Indeed he was at that time probably one of the best informed of Christians, but he was not a fighter. This is evident from the very way in which he came forward at the Council. He spoke as a man who quietly weighs up and judges all aspects of the question, and is yet deeply enthusiastic for his cause, though not for this or that one-sided detail. He spoke as a man who — I cannot say was disgusted, that would not be the right word — but as a man who felt his failure with extraordinary bitterness, for he was deeply convinced that good would come for Christianity only if the view for which he stood won its way through.

Thus he withdrew into a kind of hermitage. For the rest of his life he became a hermit, following however, in response to the inner impulses of his soul, a quite definite course of the inner life. It was that of investigating the origin of the inspiration of thought. His mystic penetration was in the effort to perceive whence thinking receives its inspiration. It became one great longing in him to find the source of thinking in the spiritual world, until at length he was filled through and through with this longing. And with this longing he died, without having reached any real conclusion, any concrete answer during that earthly life. No answer was forthcoming. The time was after all unfavourable. Then passing through the gate of death, he underwent a peculiar experience. For several decades after his death he could still look back upon his earthly life, and he saw it forever coloured by that element to which he

had come at last. In retrospective consideration starting at
the point of death he saw the human being thinking. Still
this was no fulfilment of the question. And this is most
important. There was as yet no thought in answer to the
question. But though there was no answer, he was able
after his death, to look, in marvellously clear imaginations,
into the cosmic intelligence of the universe. The thoughts
of the universe he did not see. He would have seen them
if his longing had reached fulfilment. He did not see the
thoughts of the universe, but he saw in images the thinking
of the universe.

Thus there lived through the journey between death and
new birth one who was as in a state of equilibrium between
mystic imaginative vision and his former sharp-witted thinking — a thinking, however, in perpetual flow, that had not
reached its conclusion.

In the elaboration of the karma, his mystic tendency
won the day to begin with. He was born again in the
Middle Ages as a visionary, a woman, who unfolded
truly wonderful insight into the spiritual world. For a
time the disposition of the thinker fell entirely into the
background; the quality of the spiritual vision was in the
foreground. For this woman had wonderful visions, while
at the same time she gave herself up mystically to
Christ. Her soul was penetrated, with infinite depth, by a
visionary Christianity. They were visions in which Christ
appeared as the leader of peaceful hosts, not quarrelsome
or contentious, but like the hosts of peace, who would
spread Christianity abroad by their very gentleness —
something which had never yet been realised on earth. It
was there in the visions of the nun. It was deep, intensive
Christianity, but it found no place at all in what afterwards
evolved as Christianity in its more modern form. Nevertheless during her life this nun, the seeress, came into no
conflict with positive dogmatic Christianity. She herself
grew out of it and grew into a deeply personal Christianity,
which was afterwards simply non-existent on the earth.
And thus, if I am to put it in these words, the whole
universe faced her then with the question: how should
this Christianity be realised in a physical body in a new

incarnation? At the same time, long after the seeress had passed through the gate of death, there came over her again the echoes of the old intellectualism, the inspired intellectualism. The after-effects of her visions were now permeated with ideas, if I may use this expression.

Then, seeking for a new human body, this individual became the individuality of Soloviev, Vladimir Soloviev.

Chapter Nine

'MY TEMPLE'

It is astonishing to observe how the path followed by Soloviev towards the end of his life led directly to Rudolf Steiner's anthroposophy. He was then clearly tormented by having striven so little for unification of the Church in his earlier fourth-century incarnation, when he 'withdrew into the desert' as Rudolf Steiner put it in the lectures quoted in the last chapter. The argument about dogma at Nicaea was also essentially about Church unity, to some extent resembling Soloviev's ideal, but in fact diametrically opposed to it. Soloviev was fighting for one united all-embracing Church; one all-embracing truth in philosophy; for dogmatic harmony instead of religious in-fighting or compromise; for a single tradition. It became clear to him that all these attempts at unification were abstract, senseless, even illusory ideas, deriving in fact from the dreadful influence of the Emperor Constantine, presiding at Nicaea, 'radiant in gold and jewels like the Archangel Michael' but devoid of any real wish to be a Christian and for whom a united Church was important only in that power of its unity might serve his purpose.

But towards the end of his short life Soloviev concluded that Sophia, though approaching and already close to earth, could not yet become incarnate. The human soul had not yet matured to the stage where this spiritual event could be realised, suffering as it still was from the unknown effects of seduction by Lucifer — 'the seduction in Paradise' — and so man had not developed sufficiently for Christ to occupy his soul. This communion with Sophia could not yet be achieved on earth [and cannot be until men rise to the higher plane of consciousness reached by Soloviev.]

In his day Soloviev was quote alone. He tried hard to find others who might consciously have risen above materialism (here I define materialism as the propensity to think with the physical brain alone). He thought he might find these among the poets. I think this was the basis of his love for Fet, Velichko and Sluchevsky. But the spirituality of poets is subconscious and does not necessarily lead to morality. The extent to which this distressed Soloviev can be judged from his lecture on Lermontov:

Of life after death we know nothing for sure and therefore we will not talk about it. But there is a moral law just as immutable as mathematical law, that does not allow anyone to experience after death an arbitrary transformation not justified by previous moral behaviour. If life continues after death, it can obviously do so only at the same level on which it stopped. But we know that the high quality of Lermontov's inborn genius was counterbalanced by the low level of his moral achievement. Lermontov departed with a burden of undischarged debt — for his failure to develop his wonderful God-given talent, given him as a gift. He was called upon to impel us, his heirs, in a great movement forwards and upwards towards true superhumanity, — but we received nothing from him.

This we may regret, but Lermontov's failure to fulfil his responsibility to us does not of course relieve us of our responsibility towards him. It is our duty to lighten the burden of souls of those who have passed away. In addition to Lermontov's burden of unfulfilled mission he bears another heavy load which we can and must lighten. By his beautiful presentation of false thoughts and feelings he made them and makes them attractive to the inexperienced, and if he brings even one of the least of these to take a false path, the knowledge of this, now clear and repugnant to him, must be like a heavy stone on his soul.

By exposing the falsehood of the demonism extolled by Lermontov, which can only delay people on the road to their true superhuman objective, we can at least demolish the falsehood and to some small extent reduce the load borne by that great soul.

Believe me, before speaking publicly about Lermontov, I considered what was required of me by my love for the deceased; what view I should express about his mortal destiny, and I know that here, as in all quarters, there can be only one view, based on the eternal truth essential for both present and future generations, and above all, for the deceased himself. [57]

57 *Works*, Vol. IX, p. 348 — Memorial lecture delivered in 1899 to mark the 50th anniversary of Lermontov's death.

Soloviev's sorrow for the deficiencies of poets was also clearly expressed in his humorous verse about Fet:

> Once there lived a poet
> Known to all of us,
> As he got older
> He became a silly ass. [58]

and:

> Of what has warmed our life let us make conversation —
> Of Strakhov's friendship and Fet's preferment [59]...

When Fet died Soloviev experienced profound anguish:

In Memory of A.A. Fet

> He was old and long since ill and spent,
> That he should live so long left us amazed ...
> Why then now that he is laid to rest
> Should time not leave me reconciled?
>
> He never hid his gift for crazy songs,
> He said everything he ever felt like saying ...
> Why then for me is he still so substantial?
> Why is his gaze into my soul unfading?
>
> There is a mystery here ... I still hear him call —
> Mournful groan ... trembling entreaty ...
> The irreconcilable sighs inconsolably,
> Abandoned to self-pity. [60]

[It is noteworthy that Soloviev does not criticize these poets for any dearth of poetical quality but reproaches them or complains about their imperfections as human beings. This contrasts with the modern tendency to enjoy art as something morally neutral and in this context to regard the artist also as an amoral being.

58 *Poems*, p.19.
59 *Poems*, p. 19.
60 *Poems*, p. 148.

Thus art itself is no longer considered a serious discipline. In his direct attack on the moral and human faults of artists, Soloviev affirms the principles of his philosophy of art which is touched upon in the final chapter of this book.]

In his poetry Soloviev acknowledged his past and present and expressed his future intentions:

> In the early morning mist with unsure steps
> I walked towards strange and wondrous shores.
> Dawn fought with the last stars;
> Dreams still flew and our captive soul
> Prayed to unknown Gods.
>
> In the cold light of day I go the same lonely way
> As before to an unsure destination.
> The mist has lifted and my eyes see clearly
> How hard the uphill path and how far away
> Still lies the land of my imagination.
>
> But with bold strides until midnight
> I will press on towards those cherished shores,
> Where under new stars, mountain high,
> Flaming with victory fires
> My sacred Temple awaits me. 61

[What is meant by this 'Temple' of Soloviev? It is clear that the concept includes the idea of an invisible Church as *the indivisible commonalty of all people, encompassed by an all-embracing spirit,* that is, for Soloviev — Christ. Soloviev conceived this general higher commonalty as *Sophia* who at the same time represented for him wisdom, the unique indivisible knowledge of truth, in which all is united, because just as truth is or is not, so can knowledge of truth be one alone. False knowledge is not knowledge.]

Whoever loves truth and can read may discover the origins of every book, action and lecture of Rudolf Steiner, his way to truth and wisdom, It is also manifest that Soloviev's source of inspiration was also the spiritual origin of the whole Steiner opus. He called it Anthroposophy. In his lectures Steiner imagined

61 *Poems*, p. 84.

Anthroposophy as a 'live entity requiring care'. It could also be described as the 'Way to Truth' — i.e. to Christ — and equally the 'Way to Wisdom' i.e. to Sophia, His Virgin Mother. Those who seek the way to Truth and Wisdom will find it these days only in Anthroposophy and the new arts initiated by it: the architecture, sculpture, painting, recitation and dramatic art, the art of movement (eurythmy), music and poetry.

And the developments characteristic of the early days of Christianity, and which also destroyed Soloviev's hopes, repeated themselves here. After Rudolf Steiner's death in 1925 those who surrounded him were 'tempted' to 'protect' the holy impulse — to drive towards the highest levels which Steiner had occupied, by perpetuating an organization. But such steps freeze the spiritual impulse and extinguish its inspiration.

[According to conversations of the author with the editor, the very cause which led to the failure of Soloviev's dreams of a unified church became evident among those who wanted to continue in his footsteps. Any attempt to organize and direct the religious and spiritual life of man is doomed to failure because of 'people's imperfections'. The unseen, united, higher commonalty of men cannot be enforced in the physical world, whether one calls it church or something else.

Between 1913 and 1922 at Dornach in Switzerland, on a site then named 'Bloody Hill', but now 'The Goetheanum Hill', a splendidly designed building had been erected under the direction of Rudolf Steiner. This creation of art, architecture and sculpture was dedicated to the artistic disciplines of eurythmy, speech, drama and music, imbued with the new impulses of Rudolf Steiner and his brilliant wife and partner Marie Steiner. The building was, in the author's view, Soloviev's 'sacred Temple' which had found realization as a work of art. The author often mentioned this beautiful thought in conversation, but had never written it down. But it belongs essentially to the basic ideas of this book and requires mentioning by the editor. And the further fortunes of this building demand mentioning too. It was never opened or completely finished but was destroyed by arson on New Year's Eve 1922 — 'flaming with victory fires' in Soloviev's words. As if to mock spiritual fires, arsonists set fire to this artistic creation, built of wood, and thus the 'flaming' temple was destroyed. But the building was no more than an image of the real Temple of the spiritual commonalty of mankind, which is unseen, indestructible and reserved for our future.]

The uneducated minnesingers of the Middle Ages in their tales and legends have related that 'the Chalice of the Grail was invisible' and that its secret guardian 'King John, the son of Parsifal' was still 'far in the East' i.e. not yet come to earth. But he will come to earth and then many people will see Christ in this shape, and this will unify them. And in that epoch Vladimir Soloviev will be the leader.

Chapter Ten

THE ANTICHRIST

Modest as Soloviev may have been, he must have been aware of his eminence. Although he was surrounded by the most illustrious and talented people in Russia, none of them reached a comparable level in morality, breadth of knowledge, liberality and profundity. Not only in contemporary Russia but also in the entire Christian world, since the Apostles, there had been none to equal him.

Shortly before his death, Soloviev had a frightening vision.[62] His ideal — the complete unification of the Churches — was being achieved. The entire world was harmoniously at peace under the leadership of an apparently wise and excellent Emperor — well educated, a consummate writer and orator and apparently a religious man in sympathy with all three religions and intent on their unification. He convened a Council of Churches in Jerusalem.

Soloviev describes the Emperor as the exact opposite of the Founder of Christianity. Christ was the Son of a pure virgin: the Emperor is the son of an internationally infamous woman 'of easy virtue' with far too many men with equal claims to paternity. In contrast to the behaviour of the crucified 'Lamb of God' the Emperor is full of pride and demands respect and obedience. Christ said: 'My realm is not of this world'; the Emperor declaims: 'I shall transform this world into Paradise, I shall bestow peace and riches upon you and shall make all of you content and equal one to another'. Even the profound of spirit are lulled to sleep. This is the task of the gifted magician Apollonius who uses all sorts of legerdemain and magic in the process. One could say that Soloviev's 'Antichrist' is a surprisingly detailed picture of the idols of modern civilization.

At the General Council in Jerusalem the Emperor speaks to the representatives of the different Churches. Listen to his words. One might say that the words with which he beguiles them are in fact directed at Soloviev himself. Initially, with a note of mockery in his voice, he addresses all present:

62 *Works*, Vol. X, p. 193.

Most regrettably, since time immemorial you have separated into numerous sects and parties, possibly with no one
common goal. But even though you may be unable to agree
among yourself, I hope to reconcile your divisions by my
readiness to satisfy the genuine desires of each.

He then speaks to the Catholics:

I know that for the great majority of you the most precious
aspect of Christianity is the spiritual authority accorded
to its legitimate representatives, not of course for their
personal gratification, but for the general good, in so
much as spiritual orderliness and essential discipline rest
on that authority.

    Dear Catholic brethren! How well I understand your point
of view, and how much I would like to base my state on the
authority of your spiritual paramouncy. That you should not
take my words for flattery or platitudes, we solemnly declare,
by virtue of our absolute power, that the principal bishop of
all Catholics, the Pope of Rome, is hereby reinstated on his
throne in Rome with all the earlier rights and privileges of his
title and position granted by our predecessors starting with
the Emperor Constantine the Great. *

Until shortly before, Soloviev had considered Catholics as
Christians, taking the view that all the historical deceits which he
knew so well, all the dreadful cruelties and persecutions, were so
much 'temporal dust', and that basically the Church was the
Bride of Christ. He was aware of the improbable legend of papal
origin, that the Apostle Peter had been the Bishop of Rome, of the
so-called Donation of Constantine and the False Decretals —
blatantly falsified documents on which were founded the Papal
States, the whole of Roman canonical law and the entire temporal
power of the popes. The Catholic mystery appealed to Soloviev
for a while. [The idea which fits so ill the legalistic and bureaucratic structure of the Roman Church seemed to him to resemble
the all-embracing Church of the whole of mankind. However, as
with the mystery of the Roman Bride of Christ so was the 'all-
embracing Church' no more than an illusion based on the hope

*   N.B. Constantine, not Peter or Christ. — E.G.

that by some means or other unity as such would lead the Church to become the incarnation of Sophia.

For Soloviev this was a step in the process of cognition which he had to and did, in the event, overcome. The real source of this illusion was the imagination of the superior being he called Sophia. The image came to him in a moment of enhanced prophetic consciousness, and afterwards he had to sink back into a state of mundane intellect. In that state there remained a faint memory of that earlier event which initially he had misunderstood and applied to wrong circumstances. During his life he arrived at a clearer understanding of it and in the *Story of Antichrist* he expressed his somewhat sarcastic down-to-earth views.]

All the cardinals and bishops of the Catholic Church together with most of the laity and more than half the monks accepted the Emperor's invitation to join him on the dais. Only the recently elected Pope, the reincarnated 'Peter II', did not move, together with a few of his followers. Somewhat surprised and looking steadily at the Pope sitting there motionless, the Emperor raised his voice and addressed the representatives of the Orthodox Church:

> I know that among you there are those for whom the most precious aspects of Christianity are religious traditions, ancient symbols, old hymns and prayers, ikons and liturgy. And in truth what could be more dear to the religious soul? Know ye then, my beloved Orthodox brethren, that I have this day signed statutes and allocated plentiful funds for the establishment in our beautiful imperial city of Constantinople of an international museum of Christian archaeology, for the collection, study and preservation of all kinds of ancient ecclesiastical relics, predominantly Eastern, and I ask you tomorrow to elect from your midst a commission to consider with me the measures which should be taken as far as possible to bring into line the modern rites, rules and customs with the tradition and statutes of the holy Orthodox Church.

And again the great majority of the churchmen of the East and North, half the former Old Believers and more than half the Orthodox priests, monks and laymen, with cries of joy ascended the dais, with sidelong glances at the Catholics already haughtily seated there. Only John the Hermit remained in his place, sighing deeply.

The Emperor (Antichrist) then addressed the Protestants:

My dear Christians, I know those among you for whom the most precious aspects of Christianity are personal conviction in the truth and untrammelled research into the scriptures. Today, as for the museum of Christian archaeology, I have signed an order for the establishment of an international institute for unrestricted research into Holy Scripture from every possible aspect and for studies in all associated disciplines, this institute to have an annual budget of so many million marks.

All the theologians hurried on to the dais, except Professor Pauli (the reincarnated Apostle Paul) who did not move. With his followers he moved closer to the few Catholics and Orthodox who had not been impressed by the Emperor's words and had resisted joining the majority.

The Emperor now turned to the small group of those who had not joined the majority on the dais, and asked: 'What in Christianity is most precious for you?'.

John the Hermit drew himself erect and replied gently (Andrey Bely, who had heard Soloviev himself reading *The Story of Antichrist* used to say that at these words Soloviev rose from his armchair as if he were a white candle):

Your Highness! In Christianity it is Christ himself who is most dear to us and from Him all derives, for we know that in Him is contained the entire fullness of the Godhead. And from you, your Highness, we are ready to accept any benificence if we perceive the blessed hand of Christ in your generosity. And to your question — what can you do for us, here is our frank reply: confess now before us that Jesus Christ is Son of God, made flesh, risen and to return; acknowledge Him and we will lovingly accept you as the true precursor of His second glorious coming.

I have the feeling that it is Soloviev himself throwing these words at Antichrist. Despite all the temptations which he of course experienced, he loved no one more than Christ and his divine Bride and Mother.

It is curious to note that the confession required of Antichrist by John the Hermit was no proposition to be argued about at Councils, but simply 'Confess now before us that Jesus Christ is Son of God, made flesh, risen and to return'. This supports my conjecture that Soloviev was not interested in dogma but concerned only about the truth, incarnate in Christ.

The Emperor gave no reply to John the Hermit, but his face clouded. Suddenly John stiffened in horror and exclaimed: 'Brethren, this is Anti-Christ!' Shaking with anger Pope Peter pronounced sentence — 'Anathema'. At that moment the Emperor's lackey, the magician, calls down fire and kills the 'Two Witnesses' (as in Revelation 11). But Professor Pauli, representing independent thought unassailable by the magician, restores them to life. Antichrist then summons an extemporary conclave where he causes his lackey, Apollonius the magician, to be elected Pope. The new Pope produced all kinds of sensational occult manifestations, entertaining the people with spectacles of joy and horror. He will be the last of all Popes.

It is interesting that the Jews are the first to oppose and defeat the Antichrist. They learn he is uncircumcized and therefore no Jew or descendant of David and therefore no Messiah as he claims.

A *Short Story about Antichrist* was Soloviev's last work. According to the testimony of Andrey Bely, confirming the preface to Soloviev's poetry by his nephew Sergey Soloviev, Soloviev said after he had finished reading *A Short Story about Antichrist* 'I have written this as a final expression of my views about the question of the Church'.63

It would seem to be clear enough that Soloviev finally believed no longer in the unification of the Church. He considered most of the clergy to be following Antichrist, and that the last Pope would be appointed by Antichrist. The genuine unity of the Church he expected to be created by a few real Christians, who would follow a resurrected Peter and Paul who would represent the spiritual sovereignty of man. And they would see 'the Bride, clothed in the sun's rays, with the moon beneath Her feet and a wreath of twelve stars upon Her head, and they would follow Her'.

Thus ended Soloviev's great vision of Antichrist.

63 *Letters*, p. 45.

Chapter Eleven

THE DOUBLE

[A peculiar psychological phenomenon of the 19th century was the preoccupation of many thinking people with 'doubles'. Rudolf Steiner described this manifestation as 'an encounter by a person with a "guardian of the threshold" ' preventing a crossing from terrestrial to spiritual existence pending the individual's liberation from his own imperfections and his acceptance of the truth about himself.

Usually man is incapable of this. He is filled with illusions about himself and would find it difficult to accept what in fact he is. But when confronted with important decisions it does happen from time to time that a man will partly realize his faults. Then the question arises — does he have the strength to comprehend his true self? He who cannot returns to his imperfections. His will is lacking. But he who is strong enough to see his true self as in a mirror will be able to make the better decisions. Complete experience of the double derives from unrestrained striving towards self-knowledge; the more successful this is — the more frightening. Even the bravest people try to escape this. Thus knowledge of self — the 'Double' — acts as a 'guardian of the threshold' preventing man from entering the spiritual world until he finds within himself the strength to bear the disillusion and horror of self.

R. L. Stevenson's novel *Dr. Jekyll and Mr. Hyde*, Ivan Karamazov's delirium in *The Brothers Karamazov* by Dostoyevsky, and Nietzsche's *Antichrist*, should be used as illustrations of such experiences. With Soloviev, who had spent all his life on the threshold of a higher world, this phenomenon manifested itself with particular clarity. Experience of the threshold may add to the personal shortcomings of those insufficiently mature for this inner testing. Only when a person has worked through these trials within himself can he step across the threshold to a higher plane of moral and spiritual development. The struggle within oneself gives the person the appearance of a divided personality. Soloviev's sister Maria Bezobrazova experienced this contradiction in his brother, whom she dearly loved. In her memoirs of

Soloviev's youth she refers to the shadowy sides of his character, and many of Soloviev's friends related how he had overcome '... the dark aspects of his individuality'.]

In his youth, as mentioned earlier, Soloviev had been an iconoclast, shocked his father by reading Renan and other authors, frightened holidaymakers by dressing as a corpse and later involved himself with spiritualism, investigating, as Dostoyevsky remarked '... how devils show their horns'.

Not long ago Yury Terapino wrote in the journal *Russian Thought* that Soloviev had corresponded with the Devil; that after Soloviev's death the correspondence had come into the hands of his brother Michael, who was frightfully upset about it all, destroyed it, but not before telling Ellis about it, who in turn before his death had told somebody else. Of course, this is nonsense. But even Soloviev's nephew, who loved his uncle dearly, failed to understand him in respect of Antichrist, and his brother who is supposed to have been aghast when he saw the correspondence would scarcely have talked about it to Ellis, nor would Ellis have spoken of it to others.

[Curiosity about the Devil and his horns is a characteristic feature of semiconscious experience of the threshold; the frightening realization of one's personal imperfections is reflected in the Devil's image. Soloviev may well have partly expressed his experience with the devil in his poems, but it is clear that he mentioned something else vaguely among his circle of friends. — Although the author doubted the authenticity of this information she included it in her manuscript. Who could have thought it all up, if in fact it was a fabrication? In any event — no petty spirit, and if a person of substance, why should he have concealed his identity? Furthermore this sort of disturbing experience (his brother's horror on seeing the correspondence) and sensational secrets (his brother's supposed account to Ellis) never remain secret.

In this connection, however, there exists perhaps an acceptable explanation: just as Soloviev in *Three Conversations* followed Plato's example by giving *Antichrist* the form of the imagined reading of an 'old manuscript', might not he have given 'correspondence with the Devil' the form of a literary philosophical composition, in the style of Dostoyevsky? Might not this 'correspondence' have been the expression of the internal battle with himself, with his double? Allowing this possibility, Michael Soloviev in his confusion may have deprived the world of one of the most important of Soloviev's works, a work of no less importance perhaps than *Antichrist*. Here a crucial question arises: given that Soloviev's works were not immediately printed, is it not possible that he may have given copies of this 'correspondence' to his friends, and might there not be somewhere a copy of this work which did not fall into the hands of Michael Soloviev?]

The guardian of Soloviev's threshold is, however, somewhat different from those of other people. Throughout his life Soloviev was never concerned about himself, but rather with the complete embodiment on earth of the cosmic soul in political, social and economic life, that is, throughout the whole of humanity, because he considered this soul already incarnate. This was important to Soloviev despite the many mistakes and shortcomings apparent in humanity and the fact that mankind would need to rise to a higher moral plane.

In the early stages of his development, Soloviev deluded himself that 'the embodiment of the world Soul, of the Holy Sophia, in humanity', would be possible without mankind re-quiring of itself higher moral standards, but towards the end of his life Soloviev freed himself of this delusion, describing his previous subordination to it in the image of Antichrist. The talented and theoretically very idealistic personality of Antichrist could have been Soloviev's had he not overcome his delusions and the defects of his character. In that Soloviev's Antichrist wished to make humanity happy while leaving it unchanged, he was a demon — the demon of all humanity.

I believe that the Antichrist as described by Soloviev was in effect the image of his own demonic double who remained beside him throughout his life as a tempter to provoke his weaknesses and as a mocker of his devout sentiments. Soloviev overcame his temptations through his great love for Christ. [In his *Story of Antichrist* he expressed it thus: 'The thing most dear to us in Christianity is Christ Himself'.]

The great German philosopher, Nietzsche, was a contem-porary of Soloviev, his senior by nine years, dying 13 days after Soloviev, aged about 56. Towards the end of his life he went out of his mind. In contrast to Soloviev, Nietzsche was unable to combat what appeared to him as Antichrist or his double. Soloviev projected his double on to Antichrist in order to be free and to create a purer ideal. Nietzsche tried to come to terms with his Antichrist and this identification with his own failings led him to the absurd proposition that good was evil and evil — good. Thus in the end he gained inspiration from the Demon of Darkness, whom the ancient Persians called 'Ahriman'. In his *Antichrist* Nietzsche denounces 'Christianity — the curse of humanity'.

Soloviev's attitude to Nietzsche was very negative, though he could not deny his great talent and tremendous poetic strength. There were demands from all quarters that Soloviev should clarify his attitude towards Nietzsche, who was very much in fashion at the time. And he agreed that the time was ripe but could not bring himself to accept the challenge. Eventually in the weekly journal *Russ*, in one of his serialized 'Sunday letters' of 30 March 1897, he wrote about Nietzsche under the title 'Fiction or Truth?': 'One of the most characteristic features of contemporary intellectual life and one of its most dangerous temptations is the fashionable notion of the superman'. Observing that the whole of Nietzsche's sermon is no more than an exercise in words, beautiful literature but devoid of meaningful content, he continued: 'The absolute victory of semantics over the deeper but impotent aspirations of Nietzsche's spirit were more than he could tolerate and he went mad. Thus he proved the sincerity and nobility of his character and surely saved his soul'. Soloviev concludes his letter thus: 'Conceived and morally spewed up by Nietzsche, superman, with all his emptiness and artificiality, perhaps represents the archetype, which, apart from the beauty of words, brings into the open matters and movements, false though these may be. Is it possible that the linguistic gymnastics of the Basle philosopher were just the impotent expression of a real presentiment? In that case the catastrophe which overcame is is all the more tragic and significant. *Qui vivra, verra*'.[64]

Before he died he promised Bely that they would have a proper conversation about Nietzsche, but he died without implementing his promise. As Nietzsche and Soloviev crossed the threshold of the spiritual world virtually at the same time, it is

64 *Works*, Vol. X, pp 28 — 32.

possible that a conversation did take place, not between Soloviev and Bely, but between Soloviev and Nietzsche.

It is interesting how the destiny of these two individuals crossed in the soul of Andrey Bely, disciple of Rudolf Steiner. This is a poem by A. Bely, addressed to the great anthroposophical poet Christian Morgenstern:[65]

TO CHRISTIAN MORGENSTERN
Author of 'Wir fanden einen Pfad'

You from Nietzsche, I — from Soloviev
The two of us in Steiner crossed ...
You — alive, the star of life
Flicker at me ... the indigo vault.

The star descends headlong,
Shines forth in dazzling array;
Beyond — the Promised Land, — thither —
Forty years desert wandering.

Garnet and sapphire fuse
Over the broken telescope tube ...
Thousand-winged, fire-winged world!
Europe in ashes below!

We fly above the treacherous sands,
We shine above the waste land mists ...
Anthroposophy, Vladimir Soloviev
And Friedrich Nietzsche — henceforth linked!

You — from Nietzsche, I — from Soloviev;
Henceforth together in the cosmic infinite;
You the initial light of life,
I — Christian Morgenstern's white.

[Bely, if one may put it in this way, also carried Rudolf Steiner in his soul, and the internal meeting was therefore three-cornered. Bely evinced also a fourth spirit, with he himself the

65 *New Life*, No. 394, Moscow 1918.

fifth, to create as it were an invisible council. 'Bely', the pen-name of the poet Bugayev, means in Russian 'White; light', as is the summer night in the North. 'Morgenstern' means in German the 'Morning Star'. The iridescent play on words intended by Bely is untranslatable.]

As a thinker Soloviev's thought processes were quite different from let us say, German philosophers', or at least most of those who did not indulge in 'Reason's adventure' but who followed the 'safer path' (of abstract thinking) and therefore became one-sided and biased. For instance, Kant wanted to prove that logically one could not comprehend the Higher World; he overtaxed his physical brain and approached senility at an early age. So many contradictory thinkers — Platonists, Marxists, for instance — have cited Hegel that obviously nobody really under-stands him, with the possible exception of narrow specialists, but even they never agree with one another. [Hegel took one-sided abstractions to such lengths that nobody could follow him and he disappeared from view.] Schelling may have been an exception because he broke away from the abstract and reached the spiritual world. [Soloviev avoided the risk of abstraction, refer-ring always to the spiritual world, to Sophia, Christ and God.]

Thinkers like Nietzsche, Dostoyevsky and Rozanov did not rely on pure thought and the consequences were terrifying. Nietzsche allowed Ahriman to dominate him; Dostoyevsky suc-cumbed to the demon of nationalism and all sorts of other demonisms, without completely realising it. Nationalism is a very powerful demon, to which, as history teaches us, the Pharisees succumbed, betraying their Messiah and suffering ever since from the nationalism of other peoples.

Rozanov, an original and talented thinker, but unconcerned with logic or even the elementary norms of morality, once became involved in a most peculiar situation. He used to be a regular contributor to the liberal newspaper edited by Gleb Struve, while at the same time writing under another pen-name in the extreme right-wing paper of the Black Hundred. In the latter he affirmed that Jews actually had a law of ritual murder, and that a Christian boy had been killed by Belis. (This related to the Belis case, stirring passions throughout Russia in 1913 and splitting the Russian intelligentsia into two camps, just as France was divided by the Dreyfus case). When Struve wrote that he could no longer have Rozanov writing for his paper but would give him an opportunity to justify his behaviour, Rozanov replied that only crows fly in the straight line; rational beings fly in circles. (I was told this by Dr. A. Steinberg, who visited Rozanov to discuss the matter). This shows the depth of stupidity to which a disregard of logic can lead.

Soloviev was a philosopher and kept strictly to logic; but at the same time he did not think he was creating ideas, but rather receiving them from the spiritual world.

It is surprising that Soloviev, who never tolerated overt and public manifestations of nationalism, never criticized Dostoyevsky in this connection. At the personal level, Soloviev forgave his friends, many of whom were radically 'right-wing' which at that time in Russia always went together with nationalism and often with anti-Semitism.

Dostoyevsky was one of Soloviev's closest friends whose attitude to Soloviev was one of love, even adoration. Undoubtedly they must have had many discussions on philosophical subjects and one must assume that Dostoyevsky's apparent nationalism, evident in the novels, must have come up. There were probably two separate reasons why Soloviev never made a public issue of it: Dostoyevsky was very unpopular among both left and right, and Soloviev would never attack anyone who was out of favour. At a time when Dostoyevsky was not at all understood, Soloviev was the first to acclaim his greatness as a writer, as he wrote to his cousin, Katya Romanova.[66] Secondly, Dostoyevsky's nationalism was of a special kind; it was his demon, his double. Dostoyevsky vehemently denied that he was a nationalist and an anti-Semite, although the latter was clear enough. In this respect Dr. A. Z. Steinberg wrote that Dostoyevsky's anti-Semitism was clearly due to jealousy that the Jews should be 'God's Chosen People', when he considered that it was the Russians who had God in them.

Dostoyevsky wrote about it in *The Writer's Diary*, and in *The Possessed* Stavrogin's demon, Shatov, uses nearly the same words. But Stavrogin refutes Shatov, saying: 'You reduce God to the level of an attribute of nationality', while at the same time he is instilling these ideas into Shatov. Dostoyevsky had a multitude of demons, his doubles. Verkhovensky tempts his ambition;

66 *Letters*, Vol. III, p. 80.

Kirillov — his pride. On the way to the Cross — the announcement of his marriage to Marya Timofeyevna — he rejects all these temptations, descending deeper and deeper into his subconscious mind, but he runs away from the cripple because she senses his impure thoughts and exposes them. Though he feels that she is an enchanted princess — that very being whom Soloviev served all his life — he cannot perceive her under that coarse exterior. If he had achieved all that he had intended, Marya would have become a princess and he a prince — as indeed Dostoyevsky had hoped at the start; in his early drafts he calls Stavrogin 'prince'.

Possibly even more evil a demon for man than nationalism is the demon of sexual depravity. There may be those who are virtually free of nationalism, but very few are free of Ahrimanic sexuality. The monks of Mount Athos realise it and ban even hens. Stavrogin, having apparently freed himself without much effort from nationalism, remains beholden to the demon of depravity. He seduces Dasha, but not his highest Ego — Marya Timofeyevna. Because she lacks erotic attraction he leaves her and seduces Liza. The long unpublished chapter of *The Possessed* (now available in a Paris edition) contained a virtual confession by Stavrogin of the sadistic seduction of a child, which threw a horrifying suspicion on Dostoyevsky himself. Whether there was any basis for it in fact, the chapter shows the extent to which Dostoyevsky was troubled by this demon.

Chapter Twelve

THE PROPHET

Following Soloviev one may discern three ways. But all do not lead to him. Firstly by paying insufficient attention to his last words in *The Story of Antichrist,* or by misunderstanding their meaning, one may follow not Soloviev but his double, exposed before his death in that final work. This is a way followed by those promoting unification of the churches without realizing that the motives behind it are political and self-seeking rather than religious.

Of course, Soloviev himself had no such motives, but I think they were present to a great extent in those who supported his endeavours. To this day some of those following this way continue to persuade themselves and others that the profane clerical organization calling itself 'The Church' is the true embodiment of Christ's Bride and Sophia.

The second way is that of Blok and, to some extent, Bely, as well as some other less significant poets,. The Lady Beautiful was a subject for their meditation and eulogy; they thought that they had seen Her and maybe they did catch a glimpse. Blok was primarily a poet, little given to philosophy. Somehow he confused his wife with Sophia, which was in Soloviev's view a heresy, referred to in the preface to the third edition of his verse in 1900 where he thought it necessary to remark as follows:

Two of these works require special comment: 'Exhortation to Sea-devils' and 'Three Meetings'. They might lead to my being accused of a pernicious heresy. Do they not suggest a feminine origin for the Deity? This is not the place for a philosophical argument about this theosophical question, but to preserve the reader from temptation and myself from unjust censure I feel I should make the following points:

1. The transferences to the supernatural plane of carnal/ human relationships is an abomination and can only end in disaster. (The Flood, Sodom and Gomorrah and the Satanism of recent times are all examples).

2. The worship of feminine nature for itself, i.e. as a source of equivocation and indifference just as likely to lead to lies and evil as to truth and goodness — is the height of idiocy and the main reason for the general moral flabbiness and weakness of today.

3. Such stupidity and abomination have nothing whatever to do with genuine reverence for the eternal feminine, as the long accepted perceived power of Deity, including within itself the plenitude of truth and goodness, and thereby the incorruptible radiance of beauty. [67]

Soloviev himself always perceived the highest Ego in the woman he loved. It is clear that this second course led not towards Soloviev, but away from him.

The third type of response to Soloviev, and the only one which leads to a genuine understanding of him, is the way followed by Rudolf Steiner and taught since the beginning of this century. He called this discipline 'Anthroposophy'. In early works he used the expression 'Theosophy' and that is also the title of one of his books. At that time Sophia was still in suspense, above the earth and approaching it but not yet descended and entered into man. This was Soloviev's view, expressed in his poem 'Das ewig Weibliche' in the words:

Know you then: the Eternal Feminine now
Comes to the earth in form inviolate. [68]

Soloviev was indeed a prophet, as are all true poets.

Those who studied Steiner's teachings and wanted to convert them into reality formed the Anthroposophical Society in 1913. In Russia such groups were also formed, the earliest one called after Soloviev. On Steiner's advice the second group took the name of Lomonosov, the founder of scientific activities in Russia in the 18th century.

If Christianity exists today, with Christ alive within it, the Christ of today and the One who promised to be with us for ever,

67 *Poems,* preface to the 3rd edition, reprinted in the 7th edition, Moscow 1921, p. 12.
68 *Poems,* p. 163.

I know from my experience it can be found only through the books written by Rudolf Steiner, in the art inspired by him and by Marie Steiner-von Sivers and in the schools founded by them and by those who followed them.

[This is about as far as Eugenia Gourvitch was able to check the text of her book. Soloviev's verses about Sophia:

> '... the Eternal Feminine now
> Comes to the earth in form inviolate'.

she saw as a prophecy. Soloviev was writing at the end of the last century foreseeing the appearance of Rudolf Steiner at the beginning of the present century and Eugenia sought to justify this prophecy. However, the task was too great to cover in the time she had available. She explained this to her brother in the last few days of her life, saying that her book was complete but that it contained only a third of what she had hoped to express.

These concluding pages appear to be a kind of general survey written as a farewell. One might say they are a declaration of confidence in the future of mankind. She knew her life was drawing to a close and she did all she could to express as much as possible in a few words.]

Soloviev did not systematically elaborate his conception of social relationships, probably because he had not come to any clear conclusions in that respect. The substance of his *Lectures on Theocracy* and of his speech after the murder to Tsar Alexander II points to a naivety and confusion which might have led him to think that the spiritual unification of the Church of Christ could be achieved by organizational and bureaucratic measures.

Soloviev expressed his concept of a Christian theocracy directed by Tsar, prophet and priest at the very moment when a quite un-Christian autocratic despotism was exerting its power for probably the last time, supported by the servile 'byzantinism' of the so-called spiritual leadership. And these two forces — Tsar and priest — saw to it that Soloviev the prophet was silenced. All he could do in 1881 was to give a warning of the catastrophe which would destroy Tsar, monarchy and Russian clergy in 1917. He could only prophesy, not change the future. Similarly with social life: he could forecast what would be needed, but not prescribe. In his *Lectures on Theocracy* in an exceptionally prophetic moment he included the sentence that 'every man has within himself a prophet, a priest and a Tsar'. It is as if he predicted the tripartite social organization formulated by Steiner in 1917 in his 'Threefold Social Order'.

[Steiner considered that the categorization of people by their 'conditions' — ('peasants, academics, soldiers') or into other groupings, parties and classes, should be superseded; it was not people who should be organized and divided up, but their interests. Elected representatives do not in the nature of things represent their electors but the concerns of the electors, which are of course very varied. Basically, there are three different types of concern: cultural and spiritual; economic; and all those activities where the question of rights and obligations is involved. Everybody is involved in all three, but in a different fashion. Managing a business is very different from running a school, and a legal institution differs from both the others. Therefore representation of these different interests should reflect their differences, and the social organization should similarly be divided into three parts, interrelated and interdependent and clearly representing different interests to the general benefit.

Shortcomings in public life invariably stem from false or unsatisfactory representation of interests or from poor 'division of responsibility', exemplified in the Tsar's suppression of the Russian spirit expressed by Soloviev, or where ruthless economic laws override all other concerns. As everybody is concerned with all three major divisions of interest, accentuation of one aspect leads to symptoms of social ill health which can only lead to disaster in the long run.]

Soloviev formulated his philosophical system in great detail in *A Critique of Abstract Origins,* and his ethics in *The Justification of Good.* These were only preparatory notes and some basic ideas on aesthetics for instance in a series of articles on poets. But isolated remarks in Soloviev's other philosophical works indicate he had very definite and far-reaching ideas about art.

In his *Critique of Abstract Origins* he wrote:

Apart from the uneducated masses, if there exist scholars for whom the works of Plato and Kant are no more than aimless fiction, if not utter nonsense; if there exist artists

and art critics who disdain Shakespeare and Raphael ...
then the question arises — to what purpose have the best
forces of mankind been working? [69]

Soloviev considered that if art gave pleasure only, it was
inadequate: it should transform the whole of life and conquer
death, that is why an entirely new art must arise. He wrote:

Let us suppose that a poet greater than Goethe and Shakespeare presented us, in a complex poetic work, with an
artistic, that is, truthful and objective representation of the
genuine spiritual life as it has to be, completely attaining the
absolute ideal. Even then, such an artistic miracle, never so
far achieved by any poet (in the third part of Dante's *Divine
Comedy* heaven is represented with characteristics that
may be true but which lack life and reality, a considerable
failing for which the most harmonious verse cannot compensate), in existing circumstances would be no more than
a wonderful mirage in a waterless desert, aggravating not
quenching our spiritual thirst. Perfect art has as its ultimate
objective the realization of absolute ideals, not in the
imagination, but in fact. It must inspire and pervade our
real life. If it is said that such an aim exceeds the limits
of art then the question must be asked: who set these
limits? In history we find no such limits; there we see art
undergoing modification during the process of development. One form of art reaches its limits and is discontinued
and new forms arise. All would agree that the ancient
Greeks brought sculpture to ultimate perfection; the
heroic epic and pure tragedy reached a state of perfection
where further improvement could scarcely be expected. I
would go further and not regard it as a particularly daring
prognostication to affirm that the new European peoples
have already exhausted the possibilities of improving on all
the other forms of art known to us, and if art has a future it
will be in entirely new directions. Of course the future
development of aesthetic creativity depends on the general
course of history, for art is concerned with the realization
of ideas and not their initiation and growth.

69 *Works*, Vol. VI, p. 89.

Of course one need not agree with Soloviev that Greek art achieved perfection in its various branches. Renaissance artists and sculptors might merit greater esteem. Soloviev says nothing about music, but that is not so important. Important are his thoughts about the new art of the distant future. He was demanding not only completely new forms of art but the creation of a new concept of art, serious art; frivolous art is dead according to Soloviev.

A new art has indeed taken its first steps. It is serving as an inspiration for people and mankind, educating children and playing an important part as a healing and a social force. Its development has scarcely started, but is exists, and its future depends on people. Soloviev anticipated it and as a poet gave notice of it. It is still not widely accepted and it is only in its beginnings. This new conception of the basic purpose of art was created and developed by Rudolf Steiner and Marie Steiner-von Sivers, but it was Soloviev who anticipated and prophesied its advent. This new healing art is still in its early stages; especially in social life it remains as if under cover. There was a time when it was possible to exult in its power and wholesome influence in many areas, whilst the two principals were alive and their artistic creations still in existence. The wonderful architectural creation of the original building of the Goetheanum in Dornach, with its two magnificent intersecting domes embellished with sculptures and paintings — that artistic interpretation of the spiritual temple described by Soloviev the prophet, no longer exists. Evil men destroyed it, burnt it to the ground. Only one great wooden sculpture remains, because it had not then been finished and placed in position. This sculpture, depicting Christ as 'The Representative of Humanity', is surrounded by the forces of destruction — illusion and spiritual bankruptcy, which perpetually accompany each individual and all mankind.

Contemporaneously with the construction of this beautiful building, with its twin cupolas, there arose from the limitless inspiration of the two creators its spiritual and artistic complement — the new art of eurythmy — the art of 'visible language', for the performance of poetry and the art of the living spoken word and dramatic presentation expressed poetically.

With the death of Rudolf Steiner, Marie Steiner-von Sivers found a new field into which she extended their endeavours namely the 'speech-choir', which had existed in ancient Greece but had since fallen into neglect. With her death and as a consequence of tragic temptation and the lack of the clear-sighted guidance of the two creators, the spiritual movement, the fulfilment of Soloviev's prophecy, together with the new art, was gravely retarded in its development. But its embryo is there, inspired and inspiring, growing in concealment and security, just as true Christianity grew and prospered, according to the legends of the Grail, in the invisible city of Kitezh, at a time when bishops fought for power in the pretence of being Christians.

[The text ends here. The substance of the last few sentences was conveyed to Dr. Ernst verbally in London by Eugenia Gourvitch a few weeks before her death. In all probability she dictated them later in the last few days of her life. But they express in short the abiding interest of Eugenia's life, to which she was faithful over many years.]

APPENDIX ONE

EUGENIA GOURVITCH
12.8.1905 — 7.11.1977

A biographical sketch by her brother

Eugenia Gourvitch was born on 12 August 1905 in Riga. Her father, a timber producer and merchant, was a very gentle man, extremely energetic and hardworking, entirely honest and upright, quiet, serious and full of commonsense and kindness. Her mother was in some respects quite different: extremely hospitable and affable, imaginative, interested in philosophy and politics, and very musical. Despite the different temperaments of father and mother, our family life was happy and harmonious, and the children (Eugenia had two brothers — one five years her senior, and me, five years younger) were surrounded by love, warmth and parental attention.

Eugenia's life can be divided into three periods: the first — sixteen formative years in Russia between 1905 and 1921; the second — fourteen years spent wandering between Berlin, Danzig, Warsaw, Paris and then Berlin again; and finally the third — forty-two years in London — years of maturity. Her life in St. Petersburg was filled with study, lectures, seminars, excursions and visits to museums, but most of all with absorbing the riches of Russian literature and the spirit of Russian culture. Russia and St. Petersburg, where we lived from 1906 to 1921, remained her spiritual home for the whole of her life. As with all young people in times of revolution, Eugenia developed extraordinarily quickly, despite her formal education finishing in 1921 as a result of emigration.

One of her teachers, Nikolay Pavlovitch Antsiferov, kindled in her an interest and inclination towards religion and mysticism. Born Jewish, she remained Jewish throughout her life but was attracted to Christianity, especially the Russian Orthodox Church. In 1928, during a short stay in Paris, she became acquainted with Anthroposophy and, returning to Berlin, she joined a Russian Anthroposophical group. From that time on Anthroposophy became a dominant factor in her life. Together with another member of the Anthroposophical group, Sergey Ivanovitch

Selavry, she translated into Russian the compositions and lectures of Rudolf Steiner, which until then had not been translated. She devoted every spare moment to this work. Sergey Selavry became her close friend.

In 1934 — 35, the establishment and consolidation of Hitler's regime in Germany, and the urgent need to care for her mother dying of cancer in London, obliged my sister to move to England. Apart from one or two visits to Switzerland between 1935 and 1939 her life together with Sergey Selavry was over. When the Soviet army occupied Berlin he was taken to Russia where he perished in one of Stalin's camps.

By the end of the second World War Eugenia's life had changed radically. Her father died in 1942. Her elder brother, to whom she had been particularly close, died in 1945, and at the beginning of 1946 her uncle in London died, making her one of his heirs. This at last allowed her to back financially those things which were most important and dear to her: the art of speech and drama directed and developed at Dornach by Rudolf Steiner's widow, Marie Steiner-von Sivers. Eugenia put to the test her own abilities in this field, but seems to have concluded that she could never attain the standard of excellence she demanded of herself. She concentrated all her efforts on the moral and material support of the artist Hertha Louise Sultzer-Ernst who died in 1974, and the Marie Steiner School of Speech and Dramatic Art in Germany, based on her ideas and work with Wolfgang Ernst in Dornach. In London Eugenia formed an independent English Anthroposophical group, in the hope of preserving the true original spirit of the movement.

At the same time she hoped to support the spirit of Russian culture within the framework of the Pushkin Club in London. Over many years, together with the late Maria Kullman, she organized lectures and other cultural events at the Club. On the one hand it was desirable to maintain interest in and knowledge of Russian literature and traditions among emigrants and their children, trying as far as possible to avoid Russian nostalgia for the homeland having an adverse affect on the interest in Russian culture of English members of the club. On the other hand, of course, it was essential to find a way of reconciling the old and the new in culture. Each week lectures by Club members to specially invited guests were organized, regular Russian language classes held, etc. But in order to bridge the gap between the emigrants and the contemporary exponents of culture in Russia it was absolutely essential that the Club's activities remained completely apolitical and tolerant in every respect.

Of course, such an ideal state of affairs could not last long. In the late fifties, following a visit to Russia, my sister gave a lecture at the Club about her impressions. She said that in the Soviet Union the people were thirsting for spiritual leadership which the Church, contaminated by politics, could not give, and that Anthroposophy was the only path to spiritual and religious renaissance. This was as it were a signal for certain members of the Orthodox and Catholic clergies in London to mount against my sister a vehement attack, not devoid of personal vituperation and falsehood. Many members of the Pushkin Club sided against Eugenia, who ceased to take an active part in the everyday life of the club after Maria Kullman's death.

My sister devoted the last twenty years of her life to her involvement in the work of The Phoenix Timber Co. Ltd. As Managing Director of its subsidiary — Rainham Timber Engineering Ltd. — she took it from its first beginnings to a position of generally acknowledged leadership in a newly established industry. There can be no doubt that her commercial aptitude helped to compensate for her complete lack of technical understanding and knowledge of this field. Her main strength lay in her capacity to build up an enthusiastic and loyal managerial team. She endeavoured to bring the guiding principles of Anthroposophy to bear on this commercial and industrial microcosm, but whether it was Anthroposophy or her personal enthusiasm and qualities of leadership, devotion, love of mankind and transparent honesty which brought about her success is something which as her brother and rather distant from things anthroposophical I would not like to judge.

Eugenia retired from business on her seventieth birthday and for the remaining two and a half years of her life she concentrated on writing this book about Anthroposophy and Soloviev. Until the last she worked hard, refusing to take any notice of her failing health; despite three grave heart attacks she refused to spare herself and nothing produced greater outbursts of temper than the suggestion that she should 'look after herself'.

On Saturday 5 November 1977 she came to my house in the

evening to see the television transmission of 'Boris Godunov' from the Bolshoi Theatre in Moscow and with delight and relief handed me the completed manuscript of her book in Russian, which I had promised to translate into German. This was for her the completion of her life's task, and on the following Monday she was found dead in bed; she died while reading a first draft of my translation.

Eugenia had a very strong character and a quite exceptional brain, full of love for people, a person of unique kindness and generosity. Her unbounded trust in people remained with her to the last, unaffected by disappointments or even crass dishonesty on the part of some she trusted implicitly. No doubt she had enemies, but I know that she was deeply loved and she will be badly missed by most of us who had the good fortune to know her.

APPENDIX TWO

'MISS G.'

Harry Pike, one of Eugenia's colleagues, contributed an obituary to her firm's house journal in London:

Anyone who knew Miss Gourvitch could not be anything but impressed with her depth of compassion. I think this stemmed from her vast store of knowledge. Saints and sinners, philosophers and poets, artists and artisans, geniuses and tyrants, country and continent, century by century, she knew them all and, what is more, strove to understand and learn from them.She was herself possessed of a warm and generous nature, made a perfect receptacle for this fund of knowledge acquired in a search for the truth.

Even were I possessed of the words necessary to say what I feel in my heart for Miss Gourvitch, what could I say that would suffice? She believed that every ordinary person was an extraordinary person. She believed that every child was God, and that in growing up to be an adult sometimes a little of the God was lost but it was still there somewhere. She believed that the most powerful force in the world was love and that, given a chance, this love could bridge all gaps and break down all barriers. She applied her principles to her working life. Job satisfaction was not merely a condition to be sought after for efficiency's sake. It was her guiding principle. To let her know you was to introduce her to your whole family. She wanted to and did share your joys and sorrows, tangibly but tactfully whenever necessary. How many times have we sat at her desk, hard pressed with seemingly impossible problems relating to production, delivery dates etc., to be regaled with a Russian joke or an 'I remember once' from Miss G and walk away a little later with our problems scaled down to size and on the way to being resolved. Sometimes Miss Gourvitch would forget a colleague's name; she would then let you know who she meant very graphically: 'the carpenter who grows the lovely roses'; 'the machine operator whose husband was so ill last winter'; 'the draughtsman who danced so well at the firm's dinner dance' and so on. She was boss, friend and charmer to us all. She would, I know, be happy to think that her ideals were to be taken up by those of us she has left behind. That would be her best memorial.

Memories of Miss Gourvitch provide many consolations for all who knew her. For me the most consoling thing is her own personal belief in another life. Never have I met anyone so certain of this and so unafraid of death. As I have written, her knowledge of the past was so complete, who am I, or anybody else, to say that she was wrong about the future. I would not bet against her being somewhere banging a desk or shedding a tear, the first to try to fool someone into thinking she was tough, the second because that is how she really is.

APPENDIX THREE

HISTORICAL AND BIOGRAPHICAL DETAILS
OF PERSONALITIES MENTIONED IN THE TEXT

Aksakov, Konstantin S., 1817—1860. Founder of the Slavophile Movement, to which amongst many others, Khomiakov, Samarin, Katkov, Kireyev belonged. After his death his younger brother took over the Movement.

Aksakov, Ivan S., 1823—1886, younger brother of above, gifted writer and poet. Wars between Russia and Turkey gave him opportunity to express his ideas in highly coloured patriotic speeches.

Arseniev, Konstantin K., 1837 — 1919. Lawyer and public personality. Editor of the monumental Brockhaus-Efron *Encyclopedia* in 86 volumes.

Bely, Andrey, 1880 — 1934. Pen name of Boris Bugayev. Important writer of symbolist school and close friend of Alexander Blok. Met Soloviev in 1896, met Rudolf Steiner in 1912, joined Anthroposophic Society and took part in construction of First Goetheanum in Dornach. His *Memoirs of Rudolf Steiner* are contained in book available at present only in German translation: *Verwandeln des Lebens*, Basel 1975.

Blok, Alexander, 1880 — 1921. Most important Russian Poet of this century. Considered Soloviev to be precursor of new era in life, characteristics of which he could not discern, but which, he thought, would combine Socialism with Christianity. Welcomed first revolution of 1905 and expected miracles from second revolution in 1917.

Dostoyevsky, Fedor M., 1821 — 1881. Writer and Journalist. His novels (*Crime and Punishment, The Idiot, The Brothers Karamazov, The Possessed* etc.) are classics of world literature. Started life under strong socialist influence and visited secret meetings of revolutionaries portrayed in *The Possessed*. For his participation condemned to four years hard labour in Siberia (see *Memoirs from the House of Death)* followed by military service in the ranks. This experience led to complete change of political views. Joined extreme monarchist and religious wing of Slavophile Movement.

Fet, Afanasy A., 1820 — 1895. Important lyrical poet. Towards end of his life his views became impossible and he was generally shunned by friends.

Kireyev, Alexander A., 1833 — 1910. Co-founder of Slavophile Movement. Editor of *Journal of Slav Society*. Lieutenant-General. Much involved in polemic *re* Catholic Church, position of Pope etc.

Lermontov, Mikhail Y., 1814 — 1841. A most important poet, second probably only to Pushkin. Byronesque personality, army officer with loose morals. Killed in duel by brother-officer.

Mickiewicz, Adam., 1798 — 1855. Greatest Polish writer and poet, fought for liberation of Poland from Russian and Austrian occupation. Important poems: 'Pan Tadeusz', 'Dziady' (describing his love for woman who turned him down). After the 1830/31 attempted revolution Mickiewicz was forced to join Russian Government service and move to Russia, where he acquired knowledge and love of Russian literature. 1938 moved to France — Lausanne University, Professor of Latin Literature, then College de France, Paris, Professor of Slavonic Literature. Tried to mobilize public opinion to demand liberation of Poland during war in Crimea, but died in Constantinople of cholera.

Milyukov, Pavel N., 1859 — circa 1940. Prominent historian, specializing in early Russian history. In 1905 after establishment of Duma (Parliament) became leader of 'Constitutional Democratic Party' (Cadets) and was Foreign Minister in first Provisional Government after 1917. Emigrated to France in 1918 and edited *Posledniye Novosti*, the longest established and well read Russian language daily in Paris.

Pobedonostzev, Konstantin Petyrovich, 1827 — 1907. Lawyer and statesman. In 1859 became Professor of Civil Law in the University of Moscow, and in 1865 moved to Petersburg to teach law to the older sons of Alexander II, becoming the major formative influence on the future Alexander III. As Procurator of the Holy Synod and Member of the State Council he played an important part in political life at the end of the 19th and the beginning of the 20th century. He was decidedly reactionary and pan-Slavist, believed completely in an absolute monarch, and fought with all his strength against the introduction of a constitution, trial by jury and the freedom of the press.

Rachky, Franjo, 1828 — 1894. Croatian historian, collaborating with Strossmayer, see below.

Rosanov, Vasily V., 1856 — 1919. Publicist, critic, and philosopher writing for a number of different journals. In general he was a philosopher of the idealistic Slavophile persuasion. A very original thinker, he considered that the family and family life was the basis of the culture and power of nations.

Strossmayer, Josip J., 1815 — 1905. Croatian cleric, from 1840 Professor of Theology in Djakovo; 1851 — Catholic apostolic Administrator for Serbia. Very active politically in attempts to create a South-Slav state but immediately met with the problem of Serbs being Orthodox, Croatians Catholic. Hence his forceful attempts to unify the Churches. Objected originally to the dogma of the Pope's infallibility, but withdrew his objection under clerical pressure.